Henrietta Tayler

Also by Maggie Craig

www.maggiecraig.co.uk

Henrietta Tayler

Scottish Jacobite Historian
and First World War Nurse

Maggie Craig

ISBN 978-0-9934126-3-9

Cover design by Cathy Helms of Avalon Graphics.

Typeset by 3btype.com

Printed and bound by

CPI Group (UK) Ltd., Croydon CRO 4YY

For Hetty, (if I may).

Contents

Acknowledgements

I should like to thank the helpful and knowledgeable staff of the following libraries and organizations for the generous assistance they gave me while I was researching this book: Macduff Library; Huntly Library; Special Collections, Aberdeen University Library; Folkestone Library, The Friends of Brompton Cemetery; Manchester City Council at Manchester Town Hall; the Registers of Scotland, the British Red Cross, Library of the Royal College of Surgeons of Edinburgh; the archivists of Kew Gardens, Royal Botanic Gardens, Edinburgh and the Cruickshank Botanic Gardens of Aberdeen University.

I am also indebted to the websites of the British Newspaper Archive, Scotland's People, Scotland's Places, Historic Scotland, the Royal Commission on the Ancient and Historical Monuments of Scotland (RCAHMS) and the Aberdeenshire and Moray online archaeological databases.

My grateful thanks go also to my editor, Miren Lopategui, who so brilliantly did what the best editors do.

Foreword

Henrietta Tayler was a remarkable woman. Born to wealth and privilege in the upper echelons of the Scottish gentry, she might have lived a life of ease. Instead, she chose to devote herself to scholarship, writing and helping others. She did that most notably during the First World War when she served as a volunteer Red Cross nurse.

She and her brother Alistair were prolific historians, publishing more than 30 full-length works and hundreds of articles on Scottish history. They had a special passion for the Jacobite rebellions or risings of the 18th century, when the House of Stuart fought to win back the British throne from the House of Hanover. The Taylers documented many of the colourful personalities and dramatic events of those turbulent times, bringing them all leaping off the page.

When the First World War broke out in 1914, Henrietta Tayler immediately volunteered to become a Red Cross Voluntary Aid Detachment nurse. She was not a trained nurse and never became one, although she took every opportunity to learn more about nursing and medicine. As a VAD, she served throughout the four long years of the conflict, working in some of the most dangerous corners of war-torn Europe.

She survived the shells and bullets of enemy and friendly fire and the most primitive of conditions. She nursed and comforted horribly injured and gassed

soldiers, refugee children and sick and elderly civilians
displaced by the fighting. She gave the same care and
showed equal compassion to friend and foe alike. Her
short but vivid memoir of her wartime experiences, *A
Scottish Nurse at Work*, is a remarkable chronicle of
bravery, good humour and grace under pressure.

Short in stature, Henrietta Tayler was long on
personality. An attractive dark-haired woman with
bright eyes and a ready smile, she had a keen intellect,
an inquiring mind, a mischievous sense of humour, a
kind heart, boundless energy and a strong sense of duty.
She loved life and enjoyed good conversation. When she
had to, she could rough it without a word of complaint.
In more relaxed times, she enjoyed dinner parties, the
theatre, a glass of champagne and a touch of luxury.

I became aware of Henrietta Tayler through a couple
of chance literary encounters, first coming across her
when I began to do my own research into the Jacobites
of 1745. I have John Prebble to thank for the
introduction. Using the fruitful method of working
backwards from the bibliography of his 1961 classic,
Culloden, I followed a reference to *1745 and After* and
its editors, Alistair and Henrietta Tayler.

It's a book to fire the imagination, a diary of historical
events written by someone who was there. When
Bonnie Prince Charlie landed in Scotland in the summer
of 1745 to lead the final and ultimately unsuccessful
Jacobite Rebellion, he came accompanied by only a
small group of men. They were later given the romantic

name of the Seven Men of Moidart, called after that part of the Scottish Highlands where the Rising began to gather its strength.

Colonel John William O'Sullivan was one of those seven men, at Prince Charles Edward Stuart's side throughout what became known as the Year of the Prince. I was gripped both by O'Sullivan's diary and the way Henrietta and Alistair set it in context. Their introduction and copious footnotes are informative, entertaining and witty.

Some years ago I wrote a narrative guidebook to Duff House in Banff in North East Scotland. Now a country house art gallery and cultural centre, this graceful 18th century mansion was designed by William Adam as a grand country seat for the head of the powerful, aristocratic and influential Duff family. The Taylers cropped up again here, this time as the children they were in the late 19th century. Through both parents, Henrietta, Alistair and older sister Constance were members of the Duff family.

The Taylers lived between London and Banffshire. Summers were spent at their father's childhood home of Rothiemay House, fifteen miles inland from Banff. Travelling there to research and write the guidebook to Duff House, I regularly drove past the site of the old house at Rothiemay. It wasn't hard to imagine Constance, Henrietta and Alistair bowling along in a horse and carriage to visit their grand relatives at the beautiful Adam mansion on the coast.

I could see them there, minding their manners under the stern scrutiny of Duff forbears gazing down from ornately-framed portraits in the cool marble elegance of the house. As I could see them sneaking off to play on the service stairs or letting off steam by running around the wooded policies of the extensive grounds around Duff House. Constance and Henrietta would have been in the ringlets, calf-length skirts and high button ankle boots of the time, young Alistair in a scaled-down version of gamekeepers' green tweeds, Norfolk jacket and knickerbockers.

Henrietta Tayler died a few days before I was born. In my more fey moments I've wondered if she patted me on the head as we passed, handing on the baton of that passion for Jacobites. In the course of researching this book one discovery gave me quite a *frisson*. This heroine of mine was buried in London on the very same day that I was being born several hundred miles farther north.

Henrietta Tayler lived a long, active and sociable life. The books she wrote with her brother live on, available via antiquarian booksellers and easily tracked down online. Yet, aside from in her wartime memoir, you only catch glimpses of the woman herself. I've had quite a hunt gleaning what I can, where I can. I've done my best to emulate Henrietta and Alistair by providing context and connecting up the information from other sources.

Where I've quoted Henrietta's own words, I have retained her original punctuation, spelling and capitalization. She was born in 1869, in the middle of the

Victorian era, little more than a hundred years after many of the people about whom she wrote. Like them, she often gives common nouns a capital letter. Her punctuation too has an 18th century flourish. I find her style a lovely bridge between the times she was writing about, her times and our own.

I wish I could have met Henrietta Tayler. I've spent a lot of time reading her words and finding out about her life and she's become very alive to me. I think she was warm and wise, although also not the sort to suffer fools gladly. I suspect she might have scolded me roundly for stealing time away from other projects to write about her. All the same, I think she might have secretly been quite pleased. I hope so. As she herself said about one of her books, this has been a labour of love.

Maggie Craig, 2016.

Author's Note

Tantalisingly, one of Henrietta Tayler's friends wrote after her death of her unpublished full autobiography, *My Brother and I*. Despite extensive research, so far I've not managed to find this. It's not in her papers at Aberdeen University Library, classified under her niece's married name as the Lumley-Smith papers, nor in her family's Tayler of Glenbarry papers, also in safe-keeping at Aberdeen. If anyone knows where *My Brother and I* can be found, I'd love to know. I can be contacted via my publishers at **maggiecraig@alliginbooks.co.uk**

PART I
Early Days

I

Coming Home

Our "Nor-East" corner.

It's the summer of 1882 and three very excited children are making their way from their home in Kensington to London's King's Cross Railway Station. The summer holidays are here at last and it's time to head north to Scotland. Big sister Constance is 14, younger sister Hetty is 13 and wee brother Alistair is coming up for 12. The children are travelling with their parents William and Georgina. William is a London barrister, specialising in the conveyancing of property.

Cars are beginning to appear on the streets but London is still largely a city of horse-drawn transport. Hansom cabs, brewers' drays and even buses operate on real horse-power. Once they arrive at King's Cross, the Taylers step into the modern world. The vast railway station with its glass and iron roof is a soaring monument to Victorian civil engineering. The means of transport is thrilling. The Taylers will travel north by train.

Only twenty or thirty years before, the quickest way from London to Edinburgh or Aberdeen was on one of the numerous steam packets which sailed up the east coast. Even then, it took days to complete the journey, almost a week. The train whisks you from King's Cross to Edinburgh Waverley in a mere ten and a half hours. That thirty minutes is to allow a stop at York for a spot of luncheon. No one has yet had the brainwave of adding restaurant cars to the compartments and carriages.

In 1882, *The Flying Scotsman* is the name of the London to Edinburgh train. The iconic steam locomotive which will bear that name has not yet been built. The train service is also known as the *Special Scotch Express*.

After York the train heads for Newcastle-upon-Tyne. As the steam locomotive thunders ever farther north, the magical shimmering views of the Northumberland coast unfold. Lindisfarne. Bamburgh Castle. Berwick-upon-Tweed. The Royal Border Bridge is another wonder of the modern age. Its 28 arches follow a graceful curve across the river that for centuries has defined the border between England and Scotland.

The modern border is a mile or two farther north. Like generations of homecoming Scots before and since, the Taylers raise their hands in the air and give a cheer as they cross over. The *Special Scotch Express* speeds along the cliffs. Eyemouth. St Abb's Head. The Bass Rock with its wheeling and diving colonies of gannets and puffins. Then it's on past Dunbar and the glide into Edinburgh.

The Taylers spend the night in the Scottish capital and travel on up past Dundee and Aberdeen to Banffshire the following day. The train goes via Stirling and Perth.

It's a year till work will start on the mighty project that will become the Forth Rail Bridge. Only half a day this time, and then the family steps down onto the platform at Rothiemay Station on the Great North of Scotland line. William Tayler is a director of the railway company and one of those who campaigned for the railway to be built and the track extended out here. The train is making travel so much swifter for individuals and for the transport of milk and other farm produce, giving the local economy a real boost.

Rothiemay Station has become a busy hub above the river Deveron and the solid and impressive railway bridge that spans it. This will be replaced by an even more substantial bridge but that's a few decades in the future. Nestled in the rolling green hills between the towns of Huntly and Keith, this is farming country, with fields full of waving barley and long drills of flourishing green potato shaws, hill sheep and sturdy cattle. It's 50 years until the tractor will be introduced and the larger local farms are labour-intensive *ferm touns*.

There might be a dozen people employed in each of these farm towns: horsemen, cattlemen or cow bailies, senior ploughmen, young ploughboys, shepherds, dairy-maids and the orra men, who are the jacks-of-all-trades. People work hard in all weathers and enjoy their scant leisure time. There's someone in most ferm touns who can play the fiddle, often a bagpiper too.

Charles Esson the Rothiemay House coachman is waiting at the railway station, a smile of welcome on his face. William Tayler the London barrister is the Laird of Glenbarry here, known as a fair landlord and a courteous man. Cautious though he can be, he's always prepared to listen to any grievances or suggestions for improvements. A countryman born and bred, with his own prize-winning herd of Aberdeen Angus, he's highly respected for his knowledge of cattle and cattle rearing.

The coachman drives the laird and his family the two miles and a little more along the sparkling rivers Isla and Deveron to the long-established village of Milltown of Rothiemay. The journey which began with horse-drawn transport ends with it too.

They drive past the lodge house, a turreted extrava-ganza in miniature. That's where Charles Esson lives with his wife Maggie and their six young children. On up the driveway and the butler is waiting to greet them. He's Alexander Dey. His wife is Margaret and they too have six children.

The Tayler children are eager to renew their acquaintance with the old house. At first glance it's a typical Scots Baronial pile, adorned with turrets. Look closer at this rambling building and you'll soon see that its core dates from much earlier. The old Scottish tower house is the original Rothiemay Castle. Over the centuries, successive generations have built on in the style of their own times.

Constance, Hetty and Alistair know that Mary, Queen of Scots is said to have spent a night or two in the older part of the house, way back in the 1560s. The room where she slept is always pointed out to visitors. So is the bedstead on which she rested, a solid four-poster.

The ancient stone circle of Rothiemay stands in a field no distance from the house, one of many of these Neolithic monuments which dot Aberdeenshire and Banffshire. A short walk along the Deveron brings you to Dykehead, believed by many to have been the site of a Roman marching camp.

Across the river from there and close by Rothiemay railway station, carved symbol stones are being turned up in muddy fields. The Tillytarmont stones were carved by the Picts, the indigenous people of Scotland, sometime between the 6th and the 8th centuries AD. The red granite slabs are incised with images of a goose, an eagle, a serpent, a horseshoe and one of the Picts' favourite symbols, the mirror. These are hugely exciting discoveries.

Whizz forward through time and there's more history: old ruined churches and chapels, the remnants of mysterious Catholic mass houses in out of the way places, tower houses, castles and lairds' houses.

William and Georgina Tayler are modern people, always keen to foster progress in farming, transport and education. William's also an antiquarian, fascinated by this abundance of history, historical sites and artefacts. He will pass this love of the past on to his children.

Rothiemay House, its policies, walled garden and the countryside around it must have been a wonderful place for bright and imaginative children to spend their summer holidays. No wonder Alistair and Henrietta are going to grow up to become historians.

Henrietta Tayler will spend most of her life in London but Rothiemay, Banffshire and North East Scotland will always be home. In later life, she will write with huge affection of 'our "Nor-East" corner.'

2

The Laird
of Glenbarry's Daughter

A spontaneous outburst of those kindly feelings.

Helen Agnes Henrietta Tayler was born in London on 24th March 1869, her birth announced in the columns of *The Times* a few days later. Throughout her long life she was known formally as Henrietta Tayler. To her large extended family and many friends she was always Hetty.

Constance and Hetty were born in London. Alistair was the only one of the siblings to be born in Scotland, coming into the world at Rothiemay House in the summer of 1870.

The trio's parents, William James Tayler and Georgina (sometimes Georgiana) Lucy Duff, were married in 1864, when William was 55 and Georgina was 30. They were cousins, several times removed. William was the grandson of the 3rd Earl Fife and was born at Duff House in Banff. Georgina was born in Brighton, daughter of Helen Shoolbred and Admiral Norwich Duff of the Royal Navy.

William and Georgina were supremely well connected, related to many other families in the patchwork quilt of the Scottish and Anglo-Scottish gentry and aristocracy. They passed this legacy on to their children, giving them a wide network of relatives in Scotland, London and elsewhere.

Whether they were in London or Banffshire, the Tayler children had a privileged upbringing. A snapshot provided by the census of 1871 shows they were living then in Stanhope Place in Paddington with a head nurse or nanny, her assistant, a cook, a housemaid, a kitchen maid and a footman. At the time, Constance and Hetty were toddlers and Alistair not quite one year old.

The assistant nanny, cook, housemaid and footman all came from Scotland. Although the census return doesn't specify further, it seems possible that they might have come down with the Taylers from Banffshire. The senior nanny may have been French. Although her name was Anne Frampton, her place of birth was given as Haute Orelle, an area in the French Alps. Perhaps she was the wife or widow of an Englishman.

If their nanny was French that might explain why Henrietta and Alistair (and probably Constance too, who later spent a lot of time in France) were such fluent French speakers. It was a skill that stood them in excellent stead while researching Jacobite and Stuart papers, many of which were written in that language. As an adult, Hetty spoke several languages and was always willing to learn more. She put her linguistic flair to good use as a Red Cross Voluntary Aid Detachment nurse, when she nursed in Belgium, France and Italy.

Glenbarry lies a few miles along the road from Rothiemay, a small estate occupying the narrow glen that runs between Barry Hill and Knock Hill. At a little over 1400 feet, Knock is not particularly high but its distinctive shape rises above the surrounding fields, making it a landmark for miles around.

This is a place of mossy green fields, with tumbles of cleared stones piled up in their corners. A lot of backbreaking labour had to be done before there could be much productive agriculture here, as in many other places in Aberdeenshire and Banffshire. Long famous though both counties are for prize-winning cattle and high quality produce, much of this area was once wild and rocky upland.

There was an old Barry House, which may have been a small laird's house, but it had fallen into dilapidation long before William Tayler's father bought the estate. Other than a handsome church, equally handsome associated manse and an old coaching inn, most of the dwellings scattered through Glenbarry were cottar houses, lived in by agricultural workers.

The Glenbarry estate probably didn't contribute very much to William Tayler's income. What it did give him was that status as a local laird and the right to describe himself as a landed proprietor.

His family connections gave him the rambling and comfortable Rothiemay House and its surrounding estate. Like his parents before him, William and his family occupied Rothiemay House as tenants, albeit highly privileged ones. His grandfather Alexander Duff, 3rd Earl Fife, had offered it at a peppercorn rent to his daughter Lady Jane Duff and her husband, Alexander Francis Tayler, William's mother and father.

William presided over the 360 arable acres around Rothiemay House and the nearby Rothiemay Home Farm. Twenty-six agricultural labourers and servants came under his jurisdiction, eighteen men and eight women.

The Tayler family was very much part of both polite society and rural life in Banffshire, especially after William Tayler was appointed commissioner of the extensive Duff or Fife estates in North East Scotland. Among other properties, the Fife estates in this area took in Duff House, Balvenie Castle at Dufftown and Mar Lodge near Braemar. The Duffs also had a town house in Edinburgh and another in London. Fife House stood on a prime site in Whitehall now occupied by the Ministry of Defence. Its foundations sat on several cartloads of Banffshire soil, shipped to London for that purpose.

The position as land manager took over from William's work at the London Bar, leading to the family spending more time at Rothiemay House. Even when the Taylers weren't in residence, the tenants of the Glenbarry estate and Rothiemay locals were kept up-to-date with their news. In March 1868, word flashed north from London that Georgina Tayler had given birth to a daughter. Rothiemay went wild, as the local paper reported.

On Wednesday forenoon last, a telegram from London reached Rothiemay House that Mrs Tayler of Glenbarry had been safely delivered of a daughter, at 12 Chester Square, on the previous evening. The gratifying intelligence was at once conveyed to the village and neighbourhood, and it soon became apparent that there would a spontaneous outburst of those kindly feelings which are so enthusiastically evinced on the occurrence of any event in any way calculated to promote or increase the happiness of Mr and Mrs Tayler. Flags were soon seen floating from many a house-top. The bells on the Parish Church and Town Hall were at once set a ringing merry peals, and the village artillery fired *feux-de-joie* throughout the day.

Firing their guns into the air was a feature of local celebrations at the time and not only from the local volunteers or militia, the forerunners of the Territorial Army. Brides and grooms on their way to church drove through a guard of honour of their farming neighbours standing at their road ends letting off those joyful shots.

If Henrietta's or Alistair's births called forth similar jollifications, the local paper didn't record them. Perhaps Constance's arrival was met with so much local enthusiasm because people had waited a long time for the laird to become a father. William Tayler was almost sixty by the time his first child was born.

There were more celebrations to welcome Constance into the world. The children in the local parish school were given the day off. They marched the short distance to Rothiemay House where the resident staff gave them tea, cake and sweets. Full of sugar, the young scholars skipped off home afterwards waving 'their tiny flags'. You wonder if their teachers kept a supply in one of the school cupboards to be produced like rabbits out of a hat whenever there was one of these spontaneous outbursts of joy.

All of this might strike the modern reader as almost comically feudal. Or not always so comic. This was a time and a place when one man was sent to gaol for 60 days for stealing a chicken from a hen house. Tenants were expected to defer to their lairds and landlords and the language used can sound obsequious.

On the other hand, the picture that emerges is of a good deal of genuine warmth and affection towards the Laird of Glenbarry and his family and an appreciation of their commitment to the local area. Their pattern was to head north around May and stay for several months. They often kept Christmas and saw the New Year in at Rothiemay before heading back south to London.

In William's later years, he and Georgina spent the winters in Edinburgh, where Alistair attended school and the family also had a home. Like the Duffs, the Taylers never had any shortage of places to lay their heads.

Their Edinburgh home was in Belgrave Crescent off Queensferry Road. Sitting high above the Dean Village and the Water of Leith, building started on this elegant terrace of sandstone villas in 1865. So these grand homes, an extension to Edinburgh's New Town, were quite new when the Taylers lived there.

The children's maternal grandmother Helen, widow of Admiral Norwich Duff, often came to Banffshire with them in the summer. From a Scottish family herself, she liked Rothiemay and was well-liked by the locals in return.

The Taylers had the sort of fun the gentry did, with house guests playing tennis and croquet at Rothiemay House, fishing on the Deveron and going up onto the surrounding hills to shoot, bagging deer, grouse and hare. The grouse were bred to be shot, as they still are. Pity about the hares. These fleet-footed and magical animals are thin on the ground these days.

There were responsibilities too. Apart from his work for the Fife Estates, for which he received an annual salary of £500, William Tayler sat on several county committees devoted to improvements such as better roads and more efficient farming methods. He was more generous than a lot of landowners about opening up the grounds of Rothiemay House to locals. For example, the tradesmen of the town of Keith and their families travelled the eight miles to Rothiemay House for their annual summer picnic.

Georgina took a special interest in the welfare of the old and the young, organizing literary soirées to raise money to give Rothiemay school pupils a hot midday meal in the winter. In the summer of 1882, she was the main organizer of the annual Rothiemay Flower Show, held in the village hall. People came from some distance to attend. William supplied two horses and 'a commodious vehicle' to meet those arriving by train, saving them the two-mile walk from the station: which was much appreciated when heavy rain came on.

Amidst a profusion of roses, pansies, dahlias, carnations, soft fruit and vegetables, an art show and cookery competitions showcasing haggis, Scotch broth and other culinary delights, Hetty and Alistair were in charge of a stall. Aged 13 and 12 respectively, it sounds as if brother and sister had thought up this idea themselves. You can imagine them loving the preparation as they wrote or copied out the verses and mottoes mentioned below.

> One of the most novel features was a "Post Office," at which visitors were requested to call for letters which were said to be waiting for them. The letters contained verses, mottoes &c. This establishment was under the charge of Miss Henrietta and Master Tayler.

A talent for writing and literary partnerships ran in the family. Hetty was named after one of her mother's sisters. Henrietta Duff was a novelist and poet in Victorian times. From the 1930s onwards, under the pen name of John Bonett, Constance's son John Coulson collaborated with his wife Emery Bonett on a series of popular crime and mystery novels.

The year after that Rothiemay Flower Show, William Tayler organized a royal visit to Banffshire. The visitor was the Prince of Wales, later Edward VII, the bearded king whose image adorned numerous boxes of cigars. Extensive festivities were mounted to welcome him to Banff and its twin town of Macduff. The two communities square up to each other from either side of the mouth of the Deveron, where that river flows into the Moray Firth and the North Sea.

Edward was visiting his friend Alexander Duff, 6th Earl Fife. The celebrations included a grand ball held at Duff House. William and Georgina were there, of course, as *The Banffshire Journal* reported. The newspaper rather breathlessly told its readers that several of the ladies wore tartan sashes over their beautiful gowns and that many of the gentlemen sported Highland dress. Sadly, there's no mention of whether one overseas guest donned a kilt and plaid: Count Herbert von Bismarck, son of Germany's iron chancellor Otto. The Duffs were moving in high circles.

They climbed higher still a few years later when this same Alexander Duff married Princess Louise, daughter of his friend Edward and grand-daughter of Queen Victoria. Some members of the royal family thought Louise should have married one of the princes of Europe. Queen Victoria took a more pragmatic view, recognizing that while Alexander and Louise had married for love, it didn't hurt that Alexander was 'immensely rich.'

It would be nice to think that Constance, Hetty and Alistair were allowed to see something of that grand ball. Three years later family life was shattered by the death of their father. William Tayler was 77 when he died at the Edinburgh house a few days before Christmas 1886. He'd been suffering for some years from heart and kidney disease.

William's death was registered by Alistair, who was just sixteen years old at the time. Hetty was seventeen and Constance eighteen. The idyllic childhood at Rothiemay House was over.

3

Budding Author and Historian

Living on own means.

Less than six months after William Tayler's death, the contents of Rothiemay House were sold at public auction in Aberdeen. Although he and Georgina had been tenants of the Fife Estates, the contents of the house were listed as having been the property of the late Mr Tayler. The house was stripped bare. The auctioneer's advert listed beds, piles of bedding, carpets and rugs, furniture, mirrors, crockery, wine glasses and cutlery.

Seven 'feet and hip baths' were in the sale, as were '34 stags heads and skulls.' Even four gun dogs were included. Fishing rods, tennis racquets and croquet mallets were also up for sale. Mary, Queen of Scots' four-poster bedstead went too.

There's something terribly final about all of this, an almost ruthless feel to it. You wonder if Georgina Tayler and her teenage children chose this full-scale selling up of their Banffshire home, a place that had been so special to all of them. Perhaps they were backed into a corner because Alexander Duff wanted to sell Rothiemay House. The Fife Estates were shedding several properties around this time.

On the other hand, Georgina and her children had two more well appointed homes, one in Edinburgh and one in London. They didn't need the contents of Rothiemay House. Maybe they wanted to realize their assets. Yet somehow it still doesn't feel quite right.

The family kept hold of the Glenbarry Estate. For the rest of his life, in book reviews, social columns and newspaper articles, Alistair was usually referred to as the Laird of Glenbarry. After school in Edinburgh, he went to Oxford University and should have become a barrister like his father but for some reason this did not happen. He was a leading light of the Oxford University Dramatic Society, treading the boards and working behind the scenes too. The theatre became a lifelong passion.

Hetty and Constance were privately educated. There's a strong possibility their governess might also have been French. There was a cachet in having a French (or German) governess for your children in late 19th and early 20th century Britain. Many of these governesses held a British qualification, one which Hetty herself studied for and gained when she was a young woman. This was offered via an early form of distance learning pioneered by the University of St Andrews.

British universities were only just beginning to open up to women and there was still strong opposition to the very idea of admitting female students from many academics. At the same time, others were raising their voices in support of women having access to higher education.

St Andrews, Scotland's oldest university, responded by creating the LLA, the Lady Literate in Arts qualification. Although a diploma rather than a degree, this was designed to be very close in terms of academic rigour to the MA the university awarded to successful male students. Women and girls around Britain, Europe and the world attended their local colleges or studied at home and sat the exams set by St Andrews. Examinations were held in places as far apart as Aberdeen, Bermuda, Brisbane, Cairo, London, Nairobi, Truro and Wellington in New Zealand.

The LLA scheme operated for 50 years and offered students a wide range of subjects which included English, Logic, Psychology, Maths, History, Geography, Biology, Zoology, Modern and Ancient Languages and Music.

When Hetty later applied to become a Fellow of the London-based Royal Historical Society, she listed her academic qualifications as LLA, St Andrews.

In addition to her LLA and her flair for modern languages it was her proud boast that she had a nodding acquaintance with dressmaking, carpentry, geometric drawing, chemistry, cooking and Greek. She listed her skills in that order too.

In her memoir of life as a wartime nurse, she wrote that what she had done before the war was of no interest to anybody. She did mention that she had travelled extensively, 'roughing it' in various parts of the world. In contrast, she also said that she had nursed a lot of sick relatives in her time.

That these relatives included her mother and possibly also her grandmother might seem likely. Georgina Tayler died in 1896 of a heart attack following a bout of pneumonia, at the age of 63. Georgina's mother Helen had died the year before, also in London, where the Taylers now had their main home. So Constance, Hetty and Alistair lost their mother and the only grandparent they had ever known within the space of a year, when they were all in their mid to late twenties. Despite their network of relatives and friends, the Tayler siblings must have felt very bereft.

Under her married name of Constance Coulson, (her full married name was Mrs Blenkinsopp Coulson), Hetty and Alistair's older sister grew up to become a talented artist. She was also a botanist. In February 1901, at the end of the month in which Queen Victoria died, Constance set off for two years of travel and botanical research in Korea. She sailed from Liverpool on the White Star liner *Germanic*. It's not known under whose auspices she travelled. She doesn't appear in the records of Kew Gardens, the Royal Botanic Gardens in Edinburgh or Aberdeen University's Cruickshank Botanic Gardens.

Shortly before she married in 1904, Constance published *Koreans at Home: The Impressions of a Scots-woman*, which she wrote and illustrated. Her colourful yet delicate paintings and drawings shone a light into a country few Europeans in those days had the chance to visit.

By 1901, the year Constance set off for Korea, Hetty

was head of her own household in London, living at Kensington Court Mansions with a cook and a house parlourmaid. She was 31. On the night of the census her seven-year-old cousin Francis Cathcart was visiting. Like many of her neighbours, Hetty's profession was given as 'living on own means.' In the 1911 census she was at the same address, with a different cook and house parlourmaid.

The census of 1911 was the one in which many suffragettes across Britain made their protest at the continued denial of votes for women by refusing to be counted. Hetty wasn't one of them. Like many women, she might have been a supporter of extending the suffrage but not in favour of direct action.

She and her brother Alistair were now sharing a flat. Hetty was again listed as head of the household and again listed as having private means.

Alistair gave his occupation in 1911 as writer and publisher. The twin professions may have been connected with his long professional involvement with the theatre. The brother and sister's first recorded full-length joint work wasn't published until three years later, in 1914. Produced in two hefty volumes, this was the history of their own family, *The Book of the Duffs*.

Hetty and Alistair's family connections gave them a head start when it came to research. When they were growing up in the last three decades of the 19th century, they had relatives in castles and lairds' houses across the North East of Scotland. Charter rooms and chests held a host of family papers, glittering treasure chambers for the fledgling historians. One huge resource at their disposal was the Fife Estates archive.

The *Duff House/Earls of Fife* papers are now in the Special Collections at Aberdeen University Library. There are 1300 boxes, 1300 volumes (bound letters and so on) and 500 plans. The Duffs seem to have kept every piece of paper that ever crossed their or their factors' desks. They weren't always so carefully stored as they are nowadays. One researcher who dug into the boxes and papers before Hetty and Alistair remarked of one letter that 'a mouse is away with the date.'

Ploughing their way through all this to produce the two volume *The Book of the Duffs* was an enormous amount of work. Henrietta and Alistair spent years on it, researching, reading and transcribing, and all in the days before photocopiers and scanners. The book's dedication reads:

DEDICATED TO:
'THE ONLIE BEGETTER'
THOMAS DUFF GORDON DUFF
OF DRUMMUIR
AT WHOSE SUGGESTION
THIS WORK WAS UNDERTAKEN
MORE YEARS AGO THAN
THE AUTHORS CARE
TO REMEMBER

Giving an extra extravagance to the double-barrelled surname, Mr Thomas Duff Gordon Duff was another of Alistair and Henrietta's cousins. You had a lot of those if you were a Duff. Even in the days when the number of children people had was not entirely a matter of choice, many members of this family were more prolific than most.

In the 18th century, Patrick Duff of Craigston fathered 36 children, 13 by his first wife, Anne Innes of Edingight, and 23 by his second, Mary Urquhart of Knockleith. Although several of these children died in infancy, it was a family tradition that twelve of his sons 'carried Patrick to his grave' when he died in 1731. You would hope that the children carried their poor mothers wherever they wanted to go.

As Alistair and Henrietta wrote, keeping track of such a large family could be difficult.

> Almost a complete generation must have elapsed between the birth of the eldest and the youngest child of this large family, and it is reported that the father having met a small white-haired laddie playing in the garden at Craigston, inquired, 'And wha's laddie are you?' To which the future Admiral Robert Duff of Logie and Fetteresso, fifth son, who survived and is known to us, of the second marriage, is said to have replied: 'Dinna ye ken your ain son Robbie, ye auld fool!'

Alistair and Henrietta believed that half of all the Duffs living in North East Scotland in their own time in the early years of the 20th century descended from these surviving children. Almost all married and had children of their own and the Duff name became attached to many estates in Aberdeenshire and Banffshire. There were Duffs of Hatton, Fetteresso, Drummuir and many more to add to the existing Duffs of Dipple, Braco, Balvenie and elsewhere.

The Duffs were also related through marriage to many of the other powerful families of North East Scotland: the Gordons, the Urquharts, the Abercrombies, the Hays and more. There are Duffs and Duff descendants spread out now around the world. *The Book of the Duffs* is available on several sites online, with a searchable index.

Like any family, the Duffs have had their share of heroes and villains. The family tree includes slave owners, Royal Navy captains, scholars, writers, politicians, poet Lord Byron and UK Prime Minister David Cameron.

In the 17th century, Alexander Duff of Braco had a banking house in Elgin in Moray. The building is still there. From it he extended loans to his impoverished neighbours, swooping in to foreclose when they couldn't make the repayments. He swiftly built up an extensive property portfolio. He was so notorious that one Aberdeenshire laird included him in his nightly prayers, hoping a local landmark might offer some protection. '*Dear Lord, keep the Hill o' Foudland between me and that damned Duff.*'

The Book of the Duffs details all the Duffs for whom the Taylers had records but it's much more than a book of lists. It's full of stories and anecdotes, taking in the wider history of Scotland and farther afield. One explains Alistair's unusual middle name of Norwich, which he got from his mother's father, Admiral Norwich Duff.

The admiral was only 13 and a more lowly midshipman when he served at Trafalgar in 1805. He was probably the youngest person present at the great sea battle. He got his first name from his godfather the Duke of Gordon, who was also the Earl of Norwich.

At Trafalgar, the young midshipman served under his father, Captain George Duff of the *Mars*. On the morning of the battle, George wrote a letter to his wife and childhood sweetheart, who was living in South Castle Street in Edinburgh. Hostilities began shortly after noon, so it's understandably a bit of a scrawl. There's a facsimile copy of the original in *The Book of the Duffs*.

My dearest Sophia, I have just had time to tell you we are just going into action with the combined [fleets]. I hope and trust in God that we shall all behave as becomes us, and that I may yet have the happiness of taking my beloved wife and children in my arms. Norwich is quite well and happy. I have however ordered him off the quarter Deck. Yours ever and most truly, Geo. Duff.

A few hours later Captain Duff was dead, his head shot off by a French cannonball. Two days later the boy who was to become Hetty and Alistair's grandfather wrote to his mother.

My dear Mama, You cannot possibly imagine how unwilling I am to begin this melancholy letter. However as you must unavoidably hear of the death of dear Papa, I write you these few lines to request you to bear it as patiently as you can. He died like a hero, having gallantly led his ship into action, and his memory will ever be dear.

Norwich went on tell his mother of the death in the battle of Admiral, Lord Nelson and then to ask her what she wanted him to do next. Another captain had offered him a berth on his ship but the thirteen year old who had just lost his father wrote: 'I would much rather wish to see you and to be discharged into the guard ship at Leith for two to three months.'

When young Norwich did come home he brought with him the cannonball which had taken his father's head off. *Souvenir de la guerre.* This gruesome relic became one of his grandson Alistair's most prized possessions. Raeburn painted both Captain Duff and his son and there is a handsome monument to the former in the crypt of St Paul's Cathedral in London.

The Duffs were certainly wealthy and privileged. The bargain was that in time of war they did their duty to their country. The credo was crystal clear. Do your bit. Face up to danger. Lead by example. Keep a stiff upper lip at all times and maintain coolness under fire.

These were all qualities Henrietta Tayler was called upon to display after Britain declared war on Germany in August 1914.

PART II
The War

4

Knitting for Victory

The long dreaded war has broken out.

Henrietta Tayler was in Scotland when war was declared. It seems a reasonable assumption that 'the small Scots seaside town' she mentions in the following quote was Banff. Long after Rothiemay House had been sold, she and Alistair kept a small house in Banff itself.

Brother and sister crop up in local newspaper reports, often doing good works: gifting a painting or a historical document to the town's museum or handing out prizes at local events. In August 1914 Hetty was continuing the family tradition of spending summer in Scotland.

> The beginning of the war found me in a small Scots seaside town, where for a week or two I helped with Red Cross work parties, ambulance lectures, etc., and all the paraphernalia with which staying-at-home women hoped at that period to assist the speedy ending of the war – while selfish people laid in stores of sugar, jam and tinned foods, as for a siege.

A small boy of my acquaintance was asked, "What is every one doing now?" The answer expected – as the Latin grammar used to say – was "Praying for victory," but what he actually and truthfully replied was "Knitting."

There had been a nationwide appeal for women to pick up their knitting needles, with words of rebuke for any fashionable young ladies who thought it smart to say they didn't know how to knit. We'll have to hope the less-skilled knitters quickly learned how to perform the dreaded turning of the heel and how not to make the tops of the socks so tight they acted like tourniquets.

All over Britain women got together in sewing guilds and knitting bees, producing shirts, socks, scarves and gloves for the boys at the Front, comforts for the soldiers. Newspapers reported approvingly on the meetings of these groups and picked out the role models to be emulated.

The Banffshire Journal, then as now more familiarly known as the *Banffie*, told its readers about Mrs Thomson, who lived with her grand-daughter at *The Anchorage*, Macduff, This 98-year-old lady, still fit in mind and body, was busy knitting socks for the troops. She'd done the same during the Boer War and the Crimean War. Back then she presumably also knitted a few balaclavas.

Balaclavas were urgently required during the First World War too. Soldiers in freezing trenches also needed mufflers, mittens and, above all, socks. As Lucinda Gosling explains in *Knitting for Tommy: Keeping the Great War Soldier Warm*, these were crucial in warding off the dreaded trench foot. This lavishly illustrated little book includes some patterns of the time. Once they had completed a pair of socks, knitters were instructed to soak these in linseed oil to make them waterproof before sending them off.

A huge citizens' army had quickly been mobilized. The number of men now in uniform meant the military could afford to supply each soldier only with three pairs of socks every six months. These did not last long in the cold and damp of the trenches.

The army of volunteer knitters really was needed. With the benefit of hindsight, it's clear psychological needs were being met here too, allowing those left at home to feel they were contributing to the war effort in a practical and tangible way.

You couldn't keep your husband or sons safe but you could keep them and their comrades warm. Meeting up regularly with other women with menfolk at the front must also have been a much-needed distraction in a world which appeared to have gone mad. On Tuesday 4th August 1914, the day Britain declared war on Germany, this appeared in the columns of the *Banffie*:

ARMAGEDDON

A week of anxious suspense has ended in a note of deepest tragedy. Europe is aflame. The long dreaded war has broken out. Millions of men are in movement and soon will come a clash of arms such as human history has never seen, and at the mere thought of which mankind stands appalled.

So not everyone thought it would all be over by Christmas. Maybe nobody did, that well-remembered cheerful reassurance to the folks left back home no more than heart-breaking bravado.

At the end of September 1914 the *Banffie* reported that Reims cathedral 'has been shattered, mutilated — all but utterly destroyed.' The tone of the article that follows is one of utter disbelief. Why was Europe destroying itself, slaughtering its people and laying waste to its greatest treasures?

There's a phrase we 21st century people toss around ironically: *the end of civilization as we know it*. Facing Armageddon, our forebears in 1914 really must have been terrified that such a prospect could become a reality: but they were stoical back then.

Henrietta Tayler was a perfect example. She was a practical, no-nonsense sort of woman, with a fine sense of the ridiculous. Her philosophy of how to behave in difficult times was straightforward. Keep calm, don't dwell on the negative, encourage others when they falter, get on with the job in hand using whatever tools you can find and always see the funny side.

I once said to an English colleague in the French hospital where we were busy over an old lady with bronchitis, "I have been nursing my own relations with this kind of thing all my life," to which she naïvely responded, "And did they all die?"

Hetty was 45 when the war broke out, making her three years too old for foreign service according to the rules of the Red Cross. Although her language skills and the sheer scale of the need eventually saw those rules bent, that took some time. At first she cooled her heels helping look after some of the Belgian refugees who were streaming into Britain and elsewhere in Europe. They were fleeing as their country was overrun by the advancing German army. Tales of atrocities perpetrated by German soldiers against Belgian men, women, children and even babies were lurid and legion.

It's estimated that Britain alone gave sanctuary to around 250,000 Belgians during the First World War. Although there is an online research forum on this subject, this mass movement of people is otherwise almost forgotten now. You come across the occasional reminder. A handsome plaque in Manchester Town Hall thanks the city for its kindness to the refugees between 1914 and 1919.

There's a striking painting showing Belgian men, women and children landing from boats at Folkestone. They're being greeted by a welcoming committee of local dignitaries, two children and a Red Cross nurse. The painting hangs in Folkestone Town Hall.

One newspaper report, in *The Aberdeen Journal*, reported how many Belgian women arrived in Britain without hats or jackets. 'They had simply had to seize their children and run off.'

Agatha Christie encapsulated the Belgian refugees in

one man, her brilliant detective with the highly efficient little grey cells. The fictional Hercule Poirot stayed on. Most of his real compatriots did not. All but a few hundred in Britain and the other countries which offered refuge went home after the war.

The Belgian refugees who fetched up in Banff in 1914 were confused and adrift, as might be expected, 'much troubled by unknown Scottish ways and foods.' They were all Flemish speakers and as Hetty had 'a chance acquaintance with the Dutch tongue – which is practically the same as Flemish', she was able to help and reassure them. In her usual infuriating way, she doesn't explain how she came to have that chance acquaintance.

Although tensions later arose throughout Britain between some of the refugees and locals, at the start of the war there was a huge outpouring of sympathy for Belgium. The *Banffshire Journal* called the country 'our brave little ally.' There was lots of practical help for the people who'd been driven from their homes: donations of food, clothing and bedding. All around Britain, committees were set up to help the refugees and sales of work were held to raise funds.

After helping out in Banff, Hetty did a stint helping run a hastily set-up Red Cross Voluntary Aid Detachment (VAD) hospital in southern England caring for Belgians who'd been wounded before making it to Britain. She doesn't specify where but there was a family connection with Sussex in general and Brighton in particular. Her mother Georgina had been born and brought up there.

Hetty's fluency in French as well as Flemish came in useful here, the surgeon-in-charge relying on her as his interpreter. Locals were curious about these refugees, sympathetic too. They visited them bringing gifts of cigarettes, chocolate and fruit. As Hetty noted, at the beginning of the war these luxuries were not in short supply.

She was desperate to get to the front. Many volunteer nurses were, wanting to be where they felt they could do the most good. A Mrs Tweedale [sic], speaking at a concert in aid of the Belgian Relief Fund in Turriff in Aberdeenshire towards the end of 1914, put it like this:

> If there are terrible sights and sounds on the great highway to the war, there are also very beautiful things. There are the Red Cross nurses hurrying to the front, some of them mere girls, all intent on healing, utterly indifferent to personal danger and fatigue, faithful only to duty.

Hetty's sense of duty was driving her too. She had huge sympathy for the Belgian people and how their country had been invaded and devastated. She wanted to help in the most direct way possible, by tending to the wounded.

The other side of the coin was an excitement that often bubbles below her words. She was a spinster in her 40s. She might have felt her fate was to continue to be the family member others called on in emergencies. Dependable and helpful Hetty could not plead the responsibility of a husband and children of her own.

The war held horrors but it also offered freedom, especially for women. They moved out of the home in unparalleled numbers, taking on jobs previously done by the men who had marched off to the front line. There's also a sense of adventure in Hetty's memoir. She was still young and energetic but as a woman in her 40s, old enough to expect and receive respect.

She was summoned back to Scotland to run what she describes as a small VAD/Red Cross hospital of 36 beds. Again, somewhere in Banffshire seems likely. She certainly dedicated her wartime memoir to Dr Scott-Riddell, Red Cross Commissioner for the North East of Scotland, adding that it was he who had suggested she keep some notes of her experiences.

In the sadly correct anticipation of heavy casualties, all over Britain in the autumn of 1914 arrangements were being made with existing hospitals to set aside a good number of their beds for wounded servicemen. They were often brought home by ship. In September 1914, one of the Royal Navy's fleet surgeons visited the Chalmers Hospital in Banff and 'expressed himself as thoroughly satisfied with the arrangements' for the reception of the injured. In November, Dr Scott-Riddell asked the Chalmers Hospital how many beds they could make available. By the beginning of December 1914, 40 wounded serviceman had been admitted.

The capacity offered by existing hospitals still wasn't enough, hence the establishment of the Red Cross VAD hospitals, largely staffed by volunteer nurses. VADs in the Second World War joked that those initials stood for Virgins Almost Desperate. Perhaps their First World War counterparts did too.

Famous VADs included Vera Brittain, whose memoir *Testament of Youth* chronicles the devastating effect the First World War had on her generation. Agatha Christie also worked as a VAD in Torquay, initially as a nurse and then as a dispenser. She put the knowledge she acquired of poisons to good use in her crime novels.

Many Red Cross hospitals were set up in large houses whose owners had handed them over for the duration. Duff House is not a candidate here, as it was by now a sanatarium (and that's how they spelled it) specialising in the treatment of diabetes. Insulin had not yet been discovered, so much of this treatment was based on diet. The sanatarium's medical staff did help and support the Chalmers Hospital throughout the war. This included offering expertise on how to operate the newly installed x-ray equipment.

One of the doctors at Duff House was Allan Mahood. In 1919, he published a guidebook to Banff in which he thanked Miss Henrietta Tayler for her help with information, acknowledging his debt to *The Book of the Duffs*. He also thanked Hetty for her help with the proofreading.

Banffshire had four recorded VAD/Red Cross hospitals. One was at Earlsmount, a large house in the small town of Keith, eight miles from Rothiemay. There are no surviving records or minutes but given that proximity and the existing connection between the Tayler family and the town of Keith, it's a strong contender. It was also listed at one point as having 36 beds. Later in the 20th century Earlsmount became the offices of the local Registrar of Births, Deaths & Marriages. It is now a private home.

Hetty was matron and manager of her Red Cross hospital, with one trained nurse and some VAD nurses coming in daily. Unfortunately for her, she also had to answer to a committee, 'none of whom knew anything about hospital management.' She ruefully quoted one of her historical heroes on his dislike of committees. The Marquis of Montrose was a 17th century soldier, military commander and poet, who penned the following lines on the subject:

> *My dear and only Love, I pray,*
> *That little word of thee,*
> *Be governed by no other sway*
> *But purest monarchy.*
>
> *For if Committees thou erect*
> *And go on such a score,*
> *I'll laugh and sing at thy neglect*
> *And never love thee more.*

Hetty reinforced Montrose's verse with her own comment:

He, it will be remembered, had some experience of war waged under the direction of a Committee and the successful results – to the enemy!

The committee was not to blame for one major headache in running the small hospital. Drink was too easily available at the pubs and inns just outside the grounds. Each day some soldiers 'might be expected to roll in or be brought back later, with the cheerful remark: "Here's ane o' yer lads tae ye." '

Soldiers and sailors who were regaining their health and strength could be a handful. The Chalmers Hospital had to make some extra rules to cope with them. Meals were to be taken only in a man's own ward, matron's word was law, she would decide if any visitors were to be allowed in and under no circumstances were those visitors to bring in food or alcohol. There was to be no hanging around outside the hospital after 8 o'clock in the evening, 7.30 on Sundays. Smoking was permitted, in the ward, during the hours defined by Matron. How times change.

While the drunk patients would sober up, some of Hetty's patients were suffering from what became known as shell shock and we now call PTSD, post-traumatic stress disorder.

> There was the pathetic little Welsh boy, who after a bout of furniture breaking, when he took chairs for crouching Germans and made one's blood run cold by his cries of the battlefield, was found on the floor moaning. "Kill me, Matron, do kill me – I ain't fit to live."

Balancing such chilling experiences were more comical moments. One well-educated London man had joined the Seaforth Highlanders because he fancied himself in a kilt. Drink had him stripping off, being dissuaded of the notion, only to keep coming back to the nurses in 'ever greater déshabille.' He kept apologizing but kept on doing it, five times in one evening.

An American patient had also joined a Highland regiment but confessed that he felt 'kind of bashful' in the kilt. Another man who hailed from Devon was excited to find himself in the north of Scotland. Where, he asked, was John o' Groat's house? Hetty pointed out that John o' Groat's was still 200 miles north of where they were.

Her patients had served widely. The hospital received some who had been wounded at Gallipoli. They attracted great attention from pale-skinned Scots because of their sun-tanned faces. One soldier had fought at Mons, Aisne, Armentières and Ypres. He was wounded, but as he put it — not much — at Aisne, although more seriously at Ypres.

Writing in a little book Hetty kept, he signed himself F Mortigue of the 1st Battallion KORLR, the King's Own Royal Lancaster Regiment. He recalled that before Ypres: 'The French girls in Armentières were very good to us while we were there.' Shades of one of the most famous — or infamous — soldiers' songs of the time, sung with varying degrees of bawdiness:

> *Mademoiselle from Armentières, Parlez-vous?*
> *Mademoiselle from Armentières, Parlez-vous?*
> *She was true to me,*
> *She was true to you,*
> *She was true to the whole damn army too.*
> *Inky-pinky, Parlez-vous.*

Sadly, as with her full-length unpublished autobiography, Hetty's little autograph book has also disappeared.

Recuperating soldiers who became aggressive in drink remained respectful towards the nurses who were caring for them. Henrietta faced up to a belligerent Highland soldier one night in the front hall. He was determined to go back out and give a doing to the policeman who had brought him in with cuts and bruises to his face after he'd been fighting someone else.

It took her two hours to talk him out of it. They must have made a comical pair. Like many of his comrades, the Highland soldier was very tall. Hetty was very short. She stood her ground all the same and eventually her determination won him over.

> …each time he was reminded that he could not get out without knocking me down, as the key was in my pocket, [he] invariably replied: "Oh, I wouldn't touch *ye* for the world, mem;" and, at length, quite suddenly announced, "Weel, I'll awa' to my bed, and thank ye." I feel sure he afterwards led a forlorn hope somewhere, and killed many Germans. He was, like the immortal Alan Breck, "a bonnie fighter."

Mounting a one-woman search party for another of her patients she found him ready to take on all-comers out in the street. An enthusiastic crowd had gathered round. A big burly policeman was in attendance but wasn't keen on arresting a soldier. When he suggested to Hetty that maybe the man would go with her, the soldier immediately calmed down, and did, 'meek as a lamb.'

The patients were a mixture of old soldiers and fresh-faced young recruits. Warriors though many of the latter already were, they could be naïve. One boy who'd been given leave to spend two days in Perth came back to the hospital telling everyone he was going to marry the girl he had met there in the street. Hetty gently put him right.

> Being told something about the kind of company he had obviously been keeping, he said naively: "Wal, you've been as good to me as a mother, and if you don't *want* me to marry that little gurrl, I won't," and wrote her a post card to say so!

One boy had lied about his age and spent his 15th birthday in the trenches. He asked for a cake to make up for that. At the other end of the age scale was the veteran whose battle stories went back to the Boer Wars and campaigns fought in India. A Londoner who was a patient with him joked: "Old John's best story, if you can make him tell it, is of the Battle of Bannockburn!"

Local people were generous to the wounded heroes. Often Hetty would walk into the front hall to find it 'filled with little presents, such as forty rabbits, a whole salmon, a 20 lb. roast of beef, or a haunch of venison.'

After 'two hard winters and one fine summer' running this hospital, in 1916 she at last got permission to serve abroad.

5

The Grand Ocean Hospital

Champagne and Suzanne!

Henrietta Tayler's first foreign posting from the British Red Cross was to the Belgian seaside town known as La Panne in French and De Panne in Flemish. She described it as being 'in the little bit still left of free Belgium.' A glance at the map shows that it is right on the Belgian/French border, with its twin town of Adinkerke not far away.

De Panne was home to what Hetty and everyone else at the time called an *ambulance*, the term then used in English and French for a field hospital. Its nucleus was what had been a four-storey luxury hotel on the seafront, *Le Grand Hôtel de l'Océan* – the Grand Ocean Hotel.

In peacetime, De Panne was a place where Belgian families and artists spent the summer. They enjoyed miles of sand dunes, the masses of colourful wild flowers which lined them and the interplay of light cast by sand, sea and sky.

De Panne was also home during the First World War to the King and Queen of the Belgians, Elisabeth and Albert. Born Elisabeth of Bavaria, the Queen endeared herself greatly to her adopted country, and not only by staying on throughout the war in this tiny sliver of Belgium not occupied by the Germans. The daughter of a Bavarian duke who was also an ophthalmologist, Elisabeth was a trained and experienced nurse. She worked regularly at the Ocean Hospital, nursing the patients and assisting at operations.

The king and queen had sent their three children to the safety of England. A special telephone line had been laid under the sea so the family could keep in touch. When the hospital was being set up, there were frustrating delays in securing the first pieces of equipment.

The story goes that Elisabeth asked a lady-in-waiting to phone Harrods in London and order what was required. Once Harrods had established they really did have an order from the Queen of the Belgians, they got the equipment there by sea within 48 hours, and in the middle of a war, too.

Requisitioned for the duration of that war, the *Ambulance de l'Océan* expanded into other buildings around the hotel. At its height, it grew into a huge hospital complex of 2,000 beds with six operating theatres. Many of the donations required came from the UK. The Edinburgh branch of an organization known as the Everyman Foundation was a generous contributor.

The original hotel building is no longer there. A new building named after Elisabeth, Queen of the Belgians, bears a plaque remembering the *Ambulance de l'Océan*. In her memoir, Hetty always referred to the hospital simply as La Panne.

Over the course of the First World War, La Panne became famous far beyond Belgium under the leadership of the much-admired Dr Antoine Depage. He was surgeon to the Belgian royal family and founder of the Belgian Red Cross.

In a newspaper report in March 1915, Dr Depage is recorded as having great respect for the work being done by the nurses, doctors and other staff of the Scottish Women's Hospitals. These grew out of the Scottish suffragette movement.

As elsewhere in Britain, some Scottish suffragettes advocated militancy and direct action. There were arson attacks and bombings and hunger-striking suffragettes were force-fed at Perth Prison. Other women abhorred the violence, insisting that the vote would be won by reasoned argument through public speaking, peaceful protest, pamphlets and newspaper articles.

One Scottish suffragette totally opposed to violence was Elsie Inglis, an Edinburgh doctor. When the Votes for Women movement called a truce with the Government on the outbreak of war in August 1914, Dr Inglis offered her services to the War Office. She received a dismissive reply: 'My good lady, go home and sit still.'

Treating that remark with the contempt it deserved, Elsie Inglis did the exact opposite. With her fellow members of the Scottish Federation of the National Union of Women's Suffrage Societies she set up field hospitals in France, Russia and Serbia.

By the time Henrietta Tayler met Antoine Depage,

the war had already brought him devastating personal tragedy. His wife Marie was a nurse who worked tirelessly in the creation of the hospital at De Panne. In April 1915 she crossed the Atlantic to give talks to groups in the United States about the work of the hospital and to ask for donations to keep that work going.

In May 1915, her speaking tour over, Marie Depage left New York for Europe on the *Lusitania*. On 7th May, the *Lusitania* was torpedoed by a German U-boat off the coast of Ireland. The ship sank, with the loss of almost 1200 lives. Marie Depage was one of those who drowned.

In 1919, she was honoured at a memorial service in Brussels, held jointly in memory of her and Edith Cavell, the British nurse executed by a German firing squad in 1915 for helping Allied soldiers escape from Belgium. A friend of Antoine and Marie Depage, Edith Cavell had been invited by him before the war to set up the first nurses' training school in Belgium.

It's an irony of war that it often leads to major progress in medical treatment and surgical techniques. The high number of casualties treated at the Ocean Hospital allowed for them to be grouped into wards where they could be treated by the relevant specialists. The horrors of modern warfare added the effects of poison gas to those specialities.

With no shortage of samples, the bacteriologists who worked in La Panne's laboratory carried out and wrote up research on their findings, publishing these twice each year. The *Ambulance de l'Ocean* became a centre of excellence and of enormous interest to other medical professionals, many of whom paid visits. Marie Curie spent several days in La Panne's X-ray department in 1915 in the course of her war work of setting up x-ray units at field hospitals.

Radiography was proving to be a useful diagnostic tool. X-rays could show how damaging a bullet or shrapnel had been to the surrounding nerves and muscles. Surgeons could then decide whether an operation was required or if the damage would mend itself over time.

La Panne also had a workshop in which soldiers who'd lost arms and legs were trained how to make artificial limbs for themselves and others. The hospital had a physiotherapy department too. Henrietta described this as a 'school of *meccano-therapie*, with all the newest electric and other machines for restoring the normal use of wounded and incomplete limbs.'

This was not always a blessing for the men involved. As one army doctor wrote in 1915:

> ...I have no hesitation in saying that electro-therapy, properly carried out, can return thousands of men to the front in a matter of weeks, who would otherwise have required months to recover.

On Saturdays the doctors and surgeons at La Panne gave lectures to medical staff from their own and other nearby field hospitals. These were illustrated by slides and sometimes short films of operations being performed. Sensitive throughout her wartime nursing career that she wasn't a trained nurse, Hetty jumped at the chance to learn more about medicine and surgery.

Fiercely proud of Dr Depage and the skills deployed by the doctors and nurses under his command, she cited in particular the hospital's use of Carrel-Dakin antiseptic fluid, which hastened the healing of infected wounds. This was used in tandem with ultra-violet light, which was also used to treat the potentially deadly gas gangrene caused by the bacteria in those infected wounds.

In summer 1916 De Panne experienced a brief lull in activity when the Somme offensive saw most of the fighting raging in France and not Belgium. Hetty and the other nurses had time to look up and look around. She shared a seafront villa with three other women. Their house overlooked the yellow sands of the beach and the miles of sand dunes running off from it.

She wrote that it was easy to see why artists had always been attracted to this seaside town, with that dramatic interplay of the changing light and colours of sand, sea and sky. The nurses walked along the dunes and soaked up the sun, although they sometimes longed for a few cool green trees above their heads.

> They [the dunes] were very lovely in the springtime and early summer, covered with a carpet of tiny pansies and creeping dog-roses, and again in autumn when the berries were red; but in the blazing midsummer days when there was not an atom of shade anywhere and, also when the wintry gales blew driving mist and sand into every corner, La Panne had a trying climate.

When there was time to relax, the nurses put on concerts or visited the hospital shop. This too was supplied by Harrod's and in 1916 was still able to offer treats with the smell and taste of home: soap, jams and biscuits. This little Aladdin's Cave later took a direct hit from a German bomb. The man who served behind the counter was killed and the shop destroyed.

Nurses at La Panne initially came from Britain, Canada, the US and Denmark, with only two nurses from Belgium itself. The country had been devastated and so many of its people had fled elsewhere as refugees before the advancing German army. Later in the war, Belgian nurses trained in Britain and Denmark served at La Panne.

Any lulls in the fighting were relative. The guns continued to fire on the Belgian Front and could be seen and heard from De Panne. None of that seems to have scared Hetty. She described seeing plenty of German *Tauben* aircraft — ironically, the name means *dove* — flying overhead as providing 'plenty of excitement' and aerial dogfights and naval skirmishes off the coast as 'most thrilling sights.'

This sangfroid in the face of danger might have come from the blood she shared with those forbears who fought at Trafalgar and elsewhere, although memoirs of other combat nurses betray the same excitement. Talk to men and women who've experienced war or been in cities being bombed and you meet it too. Maybe it's youthful bravado, the certainty that you're never going to die. Other people never feel quite so alive as when their lives are in danger.

Perhaps it was also the case that what Hetty was witnessing seemed quite surreal. Her descriptions do often have a dream-like quality.

> When going on duty one morning at 4.30 I saw the dim outline of a Zeppelin on its way from England, and often caught sight of the picturesque Belgian cavalry stealing along the shore in the morning mist to exercise.

Nurses may relate to her description of night duty as bringing with it 'a kind of mysterious thrill' as to what the twelve-hour shift might have in store. Most nights it brought a surfeit of reality. When a rocket hit the roof of the house near the hospital, it plunged through every floor and into the basement kitchen, exploding under the kitchen table of a family sitting at their evening meal.

They were brought to the hospital's Receiving Ward, where Hetty was working at the time. Three young girls were dead or dying by the time they reached the Ocean Hospital's casualty unit. Their parents were saved only by immediate operations. The father lost one leg, his wife both of hers. Of the whole family, only the baby in its cradle escaped injury.

Emergency operations were carried out most nights, casualties brought in after being hit by artillery fire. Usually the doctors and nurses dealt with between 10 and 20 wounded men on each occasion. When there was a direct attack on the town of De Panne, there would be many more. Hetty had wanted to work in the Receiving Ward, always preferring to be busy and feeling useful as she assisted the surgeons, but she inevitably witnessed many deaths there. She described the sadness of that.

> There were many, alas, whom we could not save, who died during or after operations, or for whom nothing at all could be done save to wash off the mud and the blood, close the tired eyes, straighten the distorted limbs and cross the weary hands.

She kept going, of course. There was work to be done. Compassionate though she was, write though she did of how seeing these dying young men tore at her heart, she belonged to that more stoical generation. Or perhaps one with no choice other than to deal with what life was throwing at it. This is how she describes one of many tragedies.

> One of our own young surgeons, when he went back to take his turn in the trenches, was brought in badly wounded and died with us.

She mourned every death of patients in her care, quietly and without drama. She wasn't the sort of woman to wear her heart on her sleeve. Besides which, there were always more wounded to be cared for.

She found humour where she could. One young French Algerian asked her to write to his father to tell him his son had died a hero. Hetty took the wind out of her patient's sails, telling him firmly in her fluent French: 'Nous ne sommes pas encore à ce point-là.' 'We're not at that point yet.' The would-be dying hero was quite put out. Snatching the time to follow up on him a few days later, she found him hale and hearty in a convalescent ward.

When Hetty herself fell ill with pneumonia, she managed to see the advantages of experiencing life from the patient's point of view. Treatment involved injections every three hours with camphor oil, strychnine and caffeine, making her feel like a pin cushion. Afterwards, she joked that though she had never been wounded in battle, she would carry forever 'the scars gained on the Belgian Front.'

Invalided home on three months' sick leave, she made it back to Belgium in half that time. She attributed her full recovery to her sturdy Scots constitution. Apart from this one serious bout of illness, she enjoyed good health throughout her long life. She returned to La Panne, proud and delighted when she was put in charge of the apparatus for applying the ultra-violet rays, taking it from ward to ward. She loved it when the French-speaking Belgian patients dubbed her *Soeur de la Lumière*, Sister of the Light.

She wore a nurse's uniform of a longish dress and a capacious white apron tied snugly around her trim waist. Nurses in those days didn't wear neat caps. A piece of white cloth secured at the nape of the neck and falling in graceful folds down their backs kept their hair away from their faces. Photographs show Hetty looking like a smiling nun. She reminded herself of the sisters of Nazareth House near Hammersmith Broadway in London.

She loved nursing at La Panne but her time there was coming to an end. The Battle of the Somme had raged in France for four months, from the beginning of July to the beginning of November 1916. The loss of life on both sides was horrific. The British lost 450,000 men, the French 200,000 and the Germans 650,000. This was the price paid for an Allied advance of only five miles.

It was now Spring 1917 and the Germans seemed to be gaining the upper hand. At the coastal end of the Western Front, their forces were drawing closer to the last remnants of unoccupied Belgium. There was a very real danger that they might capture the Ocean Hospital. It kept treating the wounded for as long as possible.

Casualties were flooding in around the clock. Many were Scots from Highland regiments. Hetty saw one group brought in on a coal cart filled with kilted soldiers rather than fuel. Many of the injured had been gassed. The effects were horrific, the men 'suffering horribly from their eyes, their lungs and hearts, from terrible nausea, and also a few days later from very painful sores.'

One Algerian officer, dying in agony from gas gangrene, grabbed Hetty's wrist and held on so tightly that he bruised her black and blue. He died shouting his last words: '*Champagne et Suzanne!*' 'Champagne and Suzanne!' His brother visited afterwards and asked if he had said anything before he died. Did Suzanne ever find out that her name was the last word on his lips?

When German forces began to shell and bombard the hospital from land and sea, an evacuation of staff and patients was hurriedly organized. When the British Red Cross pulled its nurses out, Hetty asked for permission to help Belgian refugee children at nearby Adinkerke.

The Grand Hospital of the Ocean was able to re-establish itself a few months later. The La Panne *ambulance* remained a hospital until October 1919. During the years of war, it admitted almost 20,000 wounded servicemen.

6

The Famous Mud of Flanders

He had seen and known more than any child
of his age had a right to do.

Hetty took herself to Adinkerke 'one teeming wet day
when the famous mud of Flanders was making the
roads almost impassable.' As this must have meant that
wheeled carts could make no headway, we'll have to
assume she trudged through the mud. Typically, she
doesn't dwell on the difficulty.

What she found at Adinkerke were two huts which
were little more than cow byres. At times there were as
many as 60 children in each hut, sleeping two to a bed
until they could be moved to a more permanent refuge
outside Belgium. Hetty's new charges ranged in age
from babies up to 12 year olds. Many had been brought
in by their parents because the farms or villages which
were their homes lay either on the front line or too close
to it for comfort.

She had three helpers, all of whom were also refugees.
Traumatized by her experiences before she reached
Adinkerke, the young girl who did the housework had
frequent nightmares, waking up screaming that there

were German soldiers hiding in the huts. The only way Hetty could reassure her was to get out of bed and pretend to look for the non-existent intruders.

The children were boisterous and sometimes mischievous. They must have been hard work at times but Hetty took great pleasure in caring for them. Again, her bravery and stoicism are remarkable, although she did admit that the pounding of the big guns could be 'trying to the nerves.' The danger could come from friend or foe.

The nearby British Army was bombarding the Germans with a fifteen-pounder canon, so called for the weight of the shells it fired. Mounted on a gun carriage, it was designed to be moved into place as quickly as possible but to call it light artillery would be a misnomer. Each time it was fired, the noise was deafening. The vibration was terrifying, making pictures jump off walls and books fall out of bookcases.

What Hetty called friendly shrapnel often landed on the roofs of the huts and shells only a few yards away from their front doors. The Germans were firing back, of course. With her usual stiff upper lip, Hetty wrote that you got used to the 'long-drawn scream' of incoming shells. She managed to find something positive about there being no shelter into which she could shepherd her young charges.

> The little ones were a never-ending joy and their faith in one's power to protect them from all dangers of shot and shell most touching. There was no cellar or dug-out within reach, so mercifully one did not have to get them

out of bed on raid or shelling nights – one merely sat and comforted those who woke and cried.

One twelve-year-old boy who was a refugee from Armentières always ran to her for comfort when the shelling began. When she told him he had to try not to show how scared he was in front of the younger children, he told her that unlike them he knew what the shelling meant. 'He had seen and known more than any child of his age had a right to do.'

At one point Hetty was caring for five children under two. The one she called the joy of her heart was an eighteen-month-old boy named Joseph, Sefke for short. He had spent most of his life in the cellar into which his family had retreated for safety. Pale and weak when he arrived, six weeks of regular meals and lots of fresh air transformed him.

Hetty loved it when Sefke stood on her knee and put his arms around her neck. She never married or had children of her own but loved many children and was loved by them in return. When Sefke's mother came to visit, the little boy turned to Hetty rather than to her. Thankfully, his mother found this funny rather than hurtful. The cover of this book shows Hetty with Sefke on her lap. He's almost as big as she is.

Her memoir doesn't tell us what happened to Sefke, only that all the children in her care were eventually put on a train to travel to the safety of Switzerland, hopefully with their parents. Elisabeth, Queen of the Belgians saw them off, giving each child a bag of sweets.

Hetty didn't have time to mope over her parting from Sefke. The Red Cross called her back to London. Another challenge awaited.

7

No Glamour or Romance
of War

If you can keep your head...

Hetty went home from Belgium via Boulogne in 1917
on the night following the worst air raid there had yet
been on the Channel port: which was saying something.
Boulogne-sur-mer, to give the city its full name, was a
favourite target for German bombers. Throughout the
war, huge amounts of military supplies were landed
there after the short sea crossing from Britain. If the
Germans could hit the depots in which these supplies
were stored, they could seriously hamper the British
army and war effort.

Hundreds of thousands of British troops landed at
Boulogne too, as tens of thousands of wounded servicemen were cared for in hundreds of field hospitals in and
around Boulogne, Calais and Dunkirk. Those two ports
were also important bases for British forces.

Hetty spent her night in Boulogne at the Hotel Christol,
picking her way through the devastation of the previous
night's air raid to get there. The Christol had been
commandeered in 1914, initially as a hospital. It soon

became the headquarters of the Red Cross in France and also a hostel for their personnel passing through Boulogne.

The Christol occupied a commanding position on the waterfront, opposite the busy quays of the river Liane. Built in the 19th century, it was an impressive five-storey building with wrought-iron balconies on the first floor. The façade of honey-coloured sandstone was in an elegant neo-classical style.

The Christol was equally elegant inside, all high ceilings, chandeliers and gilt-framed wall-mounted mirrors. Even through the war and the building's service with the Red Cross, old photographs show that the dining room retained its well-draped linen table cloths and vases of flowers.

At 9 o'clock on the evening Hetty was there, the air raid siren went off again. She and another nurse found their way through the blackout to the room they'd been allotted in the hotel. Even for the stoical Hetty it must have been a frightening moment. She'd seem the damage done by the previous night's raid.

Without exchanging names or being able to see each other the two women spoke deep into the night. Sleep would have been impossible anyway, with nerves jangling in anticipation of more bombs dropping from the sky. The conversation was long and interesting, although Hetty gives no further details.

Perhaps they were swapping stories of their experiences. Perhaps they were talking about their lives before the war or what they planned to do when it was finally over, if they could see that far ahead. Perhaps they were keeping each other's spirits up. In the event, there was no further raid, so they snatched a few hours of sleep.

Hetty had to leave early next morning, before it was light, so the two women never saw each other's faces. Ships that pass in the night. The Hotel Christol survived the First World War but was obliterated with many of Boulogne's other buildings during the Second.

Hetty had been recalled to London because of a shortage in the British Red Cross of nurses who spoke Italian, another of her languages. Italy had declared war on Germany and entered the war on the side of the British and French Allies in 1916. However, the progress of the fighting meant no British nurses could get permission to travel south because their safe passage could not be guaranteed. Red tape prevented her return to Belgium.

Towards the end of 1917 she was sent to a Red Cross hospital on the Franco-Swiss border, helping care for refugees who had fled the German-occupied areas of France. The nearest town was five kilometres away. She counted every step one night when she had to walk home alone in complete darkness 'on a road like glass'. She'd been seeing off some patients who were moving on, back home via Switzerland to the unoccupied part of France.

The patients not yet fit enough to be sent home were mainly very old or very young. Hetty soon found herself

in charge of the children's ward. Offering her apologies
to Kipling, she wrote her own version of *If* to describe
what that was like. Esmarch's bandage was a kind of
plaster tourniquet which had to be applied very carefully so as not to cause any damage to the patient's
underlying soft tissues.

If you can keep your head when all about you
Are howling babies, shrieking for their food,
And keep your temper when the big ones flout you
And find them jobs to do and keep them good!
If you can dress a babe in Esmarch's bandage
And make pneumonia coats from scraps of wool.
Can cut up twenty dinners with one penknife
And get them handed round while still just cool!

If you can make sick children happy
With toys made out of bits of cork and string,
Settle their quarrels, mend their clothes and love them
And still be ready for what morn may bring!
If you can wheedle towels from "Madam Lingère"
And drugs and pills after the dispenser's hours!
Beg odds and ends from all for every purpose
And keep on friendly terms with *all* the powers.

If you *like* living miles and miles from nowhere
And walking seven miles to buy a pin,
While clouds of rain and mist hide all the landscape
And any warmth and cheer come from within.
If you can answer fifty different questions
And talk three languages with equal ease,
If you are never tired and *never* grumble!
Then come out here and help the Refugees!

A new influx of patients and a staff shortage meant that Hetty found herself doing night duty for the whole hospital. It occupied a huge building which had previously been a convent. There were 100 female beds alone, divided into five wards. As usual, the redoubtable Miss Tayler took all this in her stride, although the responsibility did sometimes weigh on her.

It was a weird sensation being the only person "up" in this enormous building, with stone staircases and vast echoing corridors, and to have to minister to the wants of asthmatic and arthritic old men – many of whom could not *move* without help – in one place, of coughing and groaning old women and girls in another, while listening all the time for the cries of the children and especially of the motherless baby...

There were frequent deaths here too. Many of the patients were malnourished when they arrived. Many were suffering from diseases such as cancer and TB. The nurses did have a plentiful supply of drugs, allowing them to ease patients' final days and hours. Hetty drew a little sketch of a nun and a nurse carrying a shrouded body through the snow from the convent to the nearby chapel that served them as a mortuary. *A Sad Little Procession* can also be seen on the front cover of this book.

Some patients were in emotional distress, others suffering from what she described as mild mental illness. The infectious diseases of the time were rife: diphtheria, scarlet fever, measles, German measles, mumps, whooping-cough and erysipelas. The latter is an acute infection of the skin and is potentially fatal. Some of the nurses caught some of these illnesses from their patients. Not Hetty, though. Once again she attributed her resistance to her robust Scottish constitution.

Adding spice to the mix was a Creole cook who hated the cold weather and who, as often seems to have been the way with cooks, flung pots and pans around when she was angry. Unfortunately these missiles were usually aimed 'at the heads of meek old women cutting up the turnips and potatoes which formed so large a part of our diet.'

The work was exhausting and there 'was no glamour or Romance of War about the nursing of these poor folks'. There was some consolation for Hetty in feeling that she was making a difference to her patients, even if only in giving them those peaceful and pain-free final few days.

She quoted the motto of another hospital, not translating the French, as she often didn't in her historical works either. Like other writers of her time, she assumed that anyone reading her writing would be able to understand the language: a harmless piece of intellectual snobbery which will amuse the linguists among us.

Guérir quelquefois (alas, not often), *Soulager souvent,*
Consoler toujours.
Cure sometimes (alas not often), relieve often, console
always.

8

They Only Longed
to Get Home

A fair heart-break.

When Hetty finally got permission to go to Italy, she went via Paris. This was the only possible route, skirting round the Western Front, although the battle lines were shifting dangerously closer. She arrived in the French capital at the end of March 1918, just when the Germans had moved into position and started bombarding the city.

As she came out of the Gare du Nord the first thing she heard was what she thought was Big Bertha. In reality, there were several of these giant guns, the weapons of mass destruction of their day. Tradition has it that they were named after Bertha Krupp, heiress of the German armaments empire.

The massive canon which greeted Hetty in Paris was in fact one of a group of seven different German super-guns, soon named after their target and dubbed 'Paris Guns'. The Germans shelled the city from March to August 1918, firing from up to 50 miles away. Firing from that distance didn't do much real damage to buildings or people but the German strategy was to try to break Parisian morale. They didn't succeed.

Hetty too was unfazed by the bombardment. Nor was she very much frightened by the air raid on Paris carried out on 1st April 1918, the night before she left for Italy. She did deign to go down into the cellar of the Red Cross club with a nervous woman staying in the room next to her.

She had a fatalistic approach to all the dangers she lived through during the war. You can imagine her muttering an old Scots saying to herself. *What's for ye will no' go by ye.* By the same token, if it didn't have your name on it you'd survive another day.

Nowadays, the TGV high-speed train will whisk you from Paris to Milan and on to Florence in just over 10 hours. In 1917, it took Hetty a day and a half, fully 36 hours, to cover the 700 miles between Paris and Florence. There were several changes of trains and long waits at railway stations on the way.

She didn't expect to be long in Florence. She had volunteered to go to Verona, 150 miles farther north, close to the Italian frontline. Yet more bureaucratic delays had her spending ten weeks in Florence, nursing wounded Italian soldiers. She liked them a lot, enjoying their charm and friendliness and their gratitude for whatever kindness and care was given to them.

With some time off here, she leapt at the chance to attend medical lectures. Those on bacteriology were delivered by Professor Achille Sclavo. A doctor and researcher, Sclavo pioneered the development of vaccines against infectious diseases. This work is carried on today at the Sclavo Institute in Siena. In the early 1960s, Albert Sabin chose the Institute as the best place to produce the oral polio vaccine he developed and which had such a beneficial impact on health worldwide.

At the end of her course of lectures Hetty sat and passed a *viva voce* examination. Despite her growing experience, she still felt there was a stigma attached to not being a trained nurse, so she was delighted by her new-found knowledge and success in the exam.

Although her Italian colleagues were friendly and helpful, hours were long, food was scarce and nothing was provided for the volunteer Red Cross nurses. They had to find and pay for their own accommodation and food. Writing about the search for a room at a subsequent posting in Italy, Hetty reflected how much the war had changed priorities and attitudes.

> I thought of the shades of our maiden aunts and Mid-Victorian relatives, and the care that used to be exercised in choosing lodgings and how the respectability of the owners, the cleanliness of the rooms, the aspect, the state of the drains, etc., were all subjects of scrupulous inquiry. This time, I went from shop to shop, merely inquiring for a place in which to sleep as near my work as possible.

While on night duty she kept herself going by boiling water to make tea out of a tea tabloid. Developed by Mr Wellcome of pharmaceutical fame, these forerunners of the tea bag were standard British Army rations during World War One. Compacted tea was shaped into a small ball the size of a hard sweet and carried around in a flat tin. This could easily be slid into a uniform pocket, keeping the tea tabloids dry until you needed one. The tins were colourfully decorated with a picture of a female hand dropping one of the tabloids into an elegant cup and saucer.

Travelling to and from the hospital, Hetty was impressed by the female tram drivers of Florence. They wore 'the most feminine of uniforms – long grey coats, like dressing-gowns, and little black bonnets, embroidered with the Florentine lily.' Back home in Scotland the new female conductresses on Glasgow's trams were proudly wearing the flattering uniform designed for them, green jackets and long skirts in Black Watch tartan.

Always wanting to be where the need was the greatest, Hetty was frustrated by the delay in getting permission to head for Italy's front line. This was way up in the north of the country and along the Adriatic Coast, where Italy bordered the Austro-Hungarian Empire and the Balkans. When Italy had entered the war on the side of Britain and France in 1916, she had done so with her own agenda.

The country had been unified as a nation state rather than a collection of smaller states only since 1870, led by men like Giuseppe Garabaldi. Some Italians thought the job was incomplete. They dreamt of regaining provinces they regarded as belonging to 'unredeemed

Italy.' They wanted to wrest South Tirol, Trieste, Gorizia, Istria and Dalmatia out of the control of the Austro-Hungarian Empire. For some, this was a national crusade. That there was such a diverse ethnic and linguistic mix in these places was a complication they chose not to take into account.

The Italian campaign was hard-fought, with horrific loss of life. As Mark Thompson writes in *The White War: Life and Death on the Italian Front 1915–1919*, three-quarters of a million Italians died. It was described as a white war because so much of the fighting happened high up in the snows of the foothills of the Alps.

There was brilliant sunshine in Rome when Hetty went there to see the officials who could grant her permission to travel north. She was left cooling her heels for half of each day she spent there because of lack of communication between different departments and the fact that government offices in Rome closed from noon till 5 pm in the summer.

> However, dogged British obstinacy obtains most things, and no one could grumble at a fate which gave her two glowing June afternoons among the ruins in Rome.

She doesn't say whether she also visited the Palazzo Muti, childhood home of Bonnie Prince Charlie, or his tomb in the Vatican. Given her abiding love for Jacobite history, it's hard to imagine that she didn't take the opportunity do so. Although of course she might already have visited Rome on her travels before the war.

Once up in the north of Italy, she was sent to a field hospital run by the French in a small Italian town she does not name. Her patients were prisoners-of-war. German was another of this polyglot's languages. Unfortunately, few of her new patients spoke or even understood it. Drawn from different parts of the Austro-Hungarian Empire, there were three Hungarians, one Bohemian, two Transylvanians, two Bosnians, one Pole and several Croatians.

As most of the prisoners spoke or understood Croatian, she set about learning it. The men took great delight in teaching their nurse. They were mainly suffering from chest and heart problems, exacerbated by starvation, and were pathetically grateful for everything that was done for them. They hadn't expected the enemy to see to it that they were nursed, treated, fed and supplied with the occasional clean shirt. Or to be so kind to them while they were doing all of that.

One man used to bless Hetty every day and rub his forehead on her hand. He'd been a shepherd before the war and was, she thought, 'strangely like a sheep.'

> None of these men impressed me as being great warriors, nor as having much stomach for the present fight. They only longed to get home.

As any linguist who's spent weeks and months abroad will understand, however much you love the language of the host country, sometimes you want to relax back into your own native tongue. When Hetty felt the need to speak English she would walk up the railway line to find one of the British ambulance trains.

Also known as hospital trains, over twenty of these were shipped over to the continent from Britain during the First World War. Originally pretty basic and used to transport casualties from the front to field hospitals as swiftly as possible, they quickly became field hospitals themselves. Some had operating theatres on board.

Several went on display at their local railway stations in Britain before being transported to the continent, allowing the public to tour the facilities in the hope of receiving donations towards running costs. The ambulance trains were staffed by Red Cross and British Army nurses.

The army nurses belonged to Queen Alexandra's Imperial Military Nursing Service. Hetty described QAIMNS as 'the finest of all services'. She had wanted to train with them even before the war, her desire to become a nurse a long-standing one. They were an elite corps, admitting only single women over 25 of a high social status. She would have qualified on all three counts but circumstances prevented her from applying. Possibly she was too much needed as a nurse by her relatives.

QAIMNS had only 300 nurses in 1914 but quickly had to relax its rules because of the urgent need for more nurses. By the end of the war, there were over 10,000 army nurses. When not in the throes of nursing they wore smart little grey and scarlet shoulder capes. The corps is now known as QARANC, Queen Alexandra's

Royal Army Nursing Corps, and continues to nurse wounded servicemen in theatres of war around the world.

There were four ambulance trains in Hetty's part of Italy, waiting their turn to load up. Rather charmingly for a lady who happily described herself as a spinster, she did also speak some Italian on these little outings, indulging in a little flirting.

> On these walks, I often fraternized with Italian soldiers, who are always very friendly – and conversational – particularly so to the English, or to nurses.

After working for a year without a break, she went home in the middle of 1918 on a short leave, returning to the same hospital in Italy just as the Spanish Flu struck. This pandemic swept through an exhausted Europe and the rest of the world from 1918 into 1919. Two million civilians worldwide and 30,000 soldiers died from it. It was most virulent when it attacked adults who should have been in the prime of life, those between 25 and 40 years of age. Wartime conditions worsened its effects and although this quote from the British Red Cross website refers to Britain, the situation was the same elsewhere.

> The war created perfect conditions for flu to spread in Britain. British civilians and soldiers were physically and mentally overburdened and undernourished. Huge numbers of people were in transit, and there was overcrowding on public transport as well as in factories, offices, frontline trenches and hospitals.

Twelve men died during the first two days after Hetty's return to Italy, as well as one of the doctors. Mortality remained high despite intensive nursing care. Nurses and doctors wore eucalyptus masks to protect themselves from infection but were so busy nursing the patients that the state and cleanliness of the wards had to be left to deteriorate. Hetty wrote that her old nurse would have said the resulting mess and general grubbiness was a 'fair heart-break' but that what was really heart-breaking was to see:

> ...strong young men, poisoned through and through, burnt up with fever, fighting for their lives and passing through delirium and coma to the final collapse.

Some lives were saved by concentrating the poison in the system into one spot and drawing it out. This was horribly painful for the patient, a truly heroic remedy. It started with an injection of pure spirits of turpentine into the thigh. After 12 – 24 hours this produced extreme pain and swelling. Hot dressings were then applied to bring the abcess to a head so it could be opened and drained. This process could take five or six days and was tricky to do when so many of the patients were delirious and kept trying to take the dressings off.

Towards the end of 1918, the war was at last drawing to a close. Like a line of dominoes flicked by a finger, one event fell into the next. On 3rd November 1918, Austria signed an armistice with Italy. On the same day, sailors of the German Navy mutinied in Kiel and

Wilhelmshaven, refusing to put to sea to fight the British Royal Navy. Unrest erupted in other German cities. Fears of a Bolshevik revolution such as had happened in Russia in 1917 propelled the Allies swiftly towards the final armistice. The First World War had its official end at 11 o'clock on the eleventh day of the eleventh month, 11th November 1918.

9

We're for Blighty

Nursing prisoners in tents in the snow.

The Italians amongst whom Hetty was living celebrated, 'with flags and flowers', and children singing everywhere. She knew she was living through history but in a way, the end of the war passed her by. Even the stoical Hetty was war-weary by now.

> When the Armistice with Germany was signed I personally was too busy fighting for the lives of dying Austrians to realize quite what an epoch making event it was.

Most of her patients had been transferred to hospital in Milan soon after the Austrian-Italian Armistice. There were still wounded to be cared for elsewhere. Hetty moved on with two doctors and two other nurses to another French field hospital in what had been a big school up in the foothills of the Alps, west of Venice and east of Verona. She was given charge of a ward set up in two tents.

She found Montecchio Maggiore a difficult experience. This was made more difficult when the mountain mists began to swirl and the snow began to fall. As she drily commented: 'Nursing prisoners in tents in the snow was somewhat of a new experience for me.'

Conditions were basic, to say the least. At first the patients didn't even have lockers, with nowhere to put their milk or tea-cups down other than the rotten boards providing the tents with a makeshift floor. The cups were pretty basic too, recycled Nestlé milk tins.

Within days the ever-resourceful Hetty had somehow found small tables to go between the beds and a larger table for her to use as a rudimentary nurses' station. Once again she presided over a number of different nationalities, Hungarians, Bosnians and Czechs. The prisoners were guarded by friendly Italian soldiers, who were supposed to stand sentry at the door of the tents but usually sat by the stove chatting with the prisoner patients.

Nurses, patients and sentries kept warm however they could, the latter often by sneaking off to warm beds in their billets in the village. Two of Hetty's shorter Polish prisoners made her laugh. Their second-hand black army greatcoats were far too big and with pointed night caps on their heads, they reminded her of gnomes in a fairy tale.

Many of her patients were pretty far gone by the time they reached her tender care. She found them to be 'poor miserable objects, dying like flies, because only arriving when at the point of death.'

The one word of Hungarian she knew she would always remember was the one she wrote down as '*Fai, fai,*' which she took to mean 'it hurts.' This was closely followed by '*Nim fai!*' 'It doesn't hurt,' which the prisoners said to encourage each other to accept an injection or a poultice. She made a practical but poignant observation about language.

> I feel that after one's experiences of nursing among the Allies one inevitably knows the words for pain, hunger, thirst, sleep, the names of different parts of the body and kindred subjects in most of the languages of Europe, and quite a useful handbook could be compiled, not too large for anyone's pocket, of the absolutely necessary hospital "shop" in the languages of *all* the belligerents.

There were short phrasebooks available in different languages but none seemed entirely adequate.

> It is curious that none of the phrase books I have met give one, ready-made, any of the questions which every doctor asks one to address to new patients, which therefore one has to build up for oneself by experience, and even the sixpenny pamphlets in Russian, Rumanian and Serbian, specially designed for Red Cross workers, occupy space with elaborate lists of food, relatives, colours and the like, and such phrases as "Please remember me to your mother," and "I have a very nice dog in England," which can hardly be regarded as strictly necessary!

The patients addressed her by a variety of names. All were complimentary but some she found funny, commenting that the patient who addressed her as *Schöne Frau/* Beautiful Woman had been very delirious indeed. She was doing herself a disservice there. She was an attractive woman, with lovely eyes and a well-shaped mouth usually curved in a smile.

Her patients also called her *Liebe Schwester*/Dear Sister, *Màdama* and variations in their own languages. Eventually they all decided to address her as *Mutter*, mother in German. She loved that, moved to tears when one man expressed the feeling behind their choice on behalf of his fellow prisoners. Hetty's description of the event illustrates the code of care and kindness by which she lived.

> ...a German scholar of the party sat up in bed and with shining eyes said undeserved things that brought the tears to mine, of how they had been mothered and cared for in their sickness and captivity, and had *never* asked in vain for anything – not, I fear, strictly true. But what else could one do but one's best for them? A *malade* is always a *malade*, of whatever nationality; and weakness and misery must always appeal to one wherever found.

Sadly, she witnessed plenty of misery, writing this about a 'half Turk called Ahmed Bugaro'.

> He had meningitis as well as broncho-pneumonia, and sat up and talked in a high-pitched gabble to his own toes all one night till it was a mercy for the others when at length he died.

> All their lungs were affected and many had pleurisy as well. My days were passed in an endless round of putting

on cold packs, giving *piqûres*, cupping, wet and dry, and administering drugs and milk whenever possible. It was a moment of triumph when I felt that everyone had been washed all over at least once, and all the claw-like nails cut.

For a long time there was a death every day and every night on this ward. She found some almost unbearable to witness.

One fair-haired boy from East Austria clung to me, panting and crying, "*Schwester, Schwester, ich soll nicht sterben. Lass mich nicht sterben.*" (Sister, Sister, I should not die. Don't let me die) – and when he found it was inevitable, begged for a priest.

After receiving the Last Rites, the boy seemed comforted. Slipping into unconsciousness, he died the following morning.

British troops began passing through Hetty's mountain village. They had first been sent to Italy from the Western Front a year earlier, in the autumn of 1917, to reinforce Italian troops in their fierce fighting against the Austro-Hungarian army. Now at last, leaving hundreds of their fallen comrades behind them, they were heading home.

It made her laugh when they tried out their Italian on her and she surprised them by replying in English. Giving them a 'Good night, you do look cheery,' she got back, 'We *are* cheery Sister, we're for Blighty.'

This affectionate term for Britain and home originated

from India in the days of the Raj, a version of the Urdu word *bilayati* or *wilayati* meaning *foreign* or *European*. It became popular during the First World War. *Getting a Blighty* came to mean having the good luck to be transferred back home, often due to an incapacitating but not life-threatening wound.

After her own usual breakfast of black coffee and a piece of dry bread, it made Hetty long for Blighty too when she walked past the soldiers in the morning to be greeted also by the 'eminently British smell of fried bacon and toast.'

The house she shared with other nurses further up the mountain was warm enough but the food was terrible. She loathed the lentils which hadn't been properly cooked through and the very hard bread. She was so hungry she resorted to soaking the bread in hot water to make what she described as chicken food. Before the war she hadn't been much of a fan of condensed milk but now really appreciated it on those rare occasions when it came her way.

The French surgeon-in-chief then asked Hetty and another British nurse to return to the town they had worked in before their deployment in the mountains. The hospital there had an influx of sick soldiers, most of them suffering from the Spanish Flu. Neither woman wanted to go. There was now a British command headquarters where they were and they were enjoying having the occasional cup of tea and conversation with the British officers, and not only them.

There were also Sunday services in a tent opposite the canteen, where we could sometimes exchange views on things in general, and English news with our *compatriotes* the canteen ladies. They enjoyed British rations, but were somewhat worse lodged than we and worked nearly as long hours.

These mobile 'expeditionary' canteens had first been set up and sent out in 1915. They were the forerunners of the NAAFI, the army's catering corps. So these British canteen ladies taking their tea and toast-making skills to the Italian Front were another group of unsung heroines of the First World War.

Reluctant to lose the boost this congenial company gave them, Hetty and her colleague nevertheless agreed to move on. The French surgeon-in-chief was very charming, told them how much he hated to lose them but that they really were desperately needed elsewhere.

With their tongues very firmly in their cheeks, the two nurses decided 'to uphold the best traditions of the British Empire and the Nursing profession.' Hetty was glad she had such a small amount of luggage. She had made it a policy throughout the war to have no more than she could comfortably carry herself.

Blood-letting was still being used as a treatment. Practised by doctors since ancient times in the belief that many illnesses were due to a plethora or overabundance of blood, this involved cutting the patient, usually in the forearm, and draining off some blood. As practised on a man with bronchitis and heart problems, this was another surreal moment in a war which had been full of them.

> About eleven I fetched the *médicin de garde* and he determined to perform blood-letting on the cardiac-bronchitic man. The lighting of the huge lofty ward was only provided for by two very much exhausted and distant electric lamps, so the operation was carried out by the light of one candle, perilously held by the carpenter in very close proximity to the tumbling locks of the operating doctor, and I was momentarily expecting a fizzle! The doctor arrived without a white coat and asked me to pin a sheet around him, more to protect his pale blue uniform from accidents than with any idea of asepsis. If the whole thing had not been a tragedy it would have been quaintly reminiscent of nursery theatricals.

The procedure gave the patient some relief but it was only temporary. He died an hour later.

Hetty liked the French patients, finding them friendly and amiable and admiring their bonhomie under pressure. One other national stereotype held up. 'When almost at the last gasp they would wish one "bon appétit" when one left them for a short time at mid-day or in the evening.' In support of her view that the French are a very polite people, she noted an interesting difference in how different nationalities opened a conversation with a woman.

> The English man or boy on friendly terms with you begins "I say." The Italian says "*Senta*" – "Listen" – for fear you might not otherwise do so, but the Frenchman invariably

begins with "*Dites, mademoiselle*," or "*Dites, ma soeur*," implying that what he really wants to hear is *your* opinion of the matter in hand.

The patients were very curious about her, wanting to know about her family and home and why she had volunteered to nurse so far away from her own country. They admired that, as they admired that she could make herself understood in so many languages. Language continued to fascinate and delight her. One Austrian sergeant to whom she had to give horrible tasting medicine always said very politely in response: "*Ich küss' Ihr die Hände.*" (I kiss your hands.)

It was now December 1918 and she was aware of a growing "*fin de guerre*" atmosphere. Now that the war had finally ended, doctors went home on leave and didn't come back, orderlies were drafted back to their military duties. Hetty was left with whoever was still there. The hospital carpenter was drafted in to help her over a few nights, tending to and witnessing the last moments of patients whose coffins he would be making the following morning.

Christmas Eve and Christmas Day 1918 were as busy as ever and there was a mass on Christmas morning which Hetty attended and appreciated, although she missed singing familiar carols such as *Hark! The Herald Angels Sing* and *O, Come all ye Faithful*.

There were some treats: music, champagne and oranges. She liberated two bottles of fizz to share out among her own patients and got her own unexpected treat later that evening. At 8 o'clock on the evening of Christmas Day, with the patients settled for the night, she was picked up and driven out to dine with the local Red Cross commissioner.

Dressing for dinner had taken on a new meaning. She wore her nurse's uniform, pleased she still had one apron which had been properly laundered when she'd been back home in Britain earlier in the year. The ones she wore in Italy had been washed without soap on a stone in the local river. Over the weeks and months they had grown greyer and greyer. As she wrote at the time:

> How odd it will be when we return to civil life and shall no longer feel fully dressed for opera box or dinner party by merely putting on a clean veil and apron! I for one shall be quite sorry – it is so simple.

There were festivities for New Year's Eve too, a party organized by the local priest for the children of the neighbourhood, with games, refreshments and music played on a wind-up gramophone. Hetty loved it, as she always did love being with children.

Tired that evening, she decided not to stay up to see the New Year in. As a Scot, for whom welcoming the New Year is so important, she must have been really exhausted to make that decision. Fate stepped in. She was called before midnight to attend to a patient, so she heard the church bells ringing in 1919 after all.

She had been through so much, witnessed so much death and suffering, done her utmost to ease and relieve.

What mixed feelings she must have had as she stood listening to the bells, welcoming the first full year of peace after four years of war.

She began her long journey home by first travelling east. She crossed Venice's two lagoons at sunrise, drinking in the beauty of the view. Yet the scars of war were everywhere: blown-up bridges, churches and historic buildings.

The beautiful old town of Gorizia was in a sorry state. Now in Slovenia, back then it was known to German speakers as Görz. It lay on the Adriatic coast on the border between the Austro-Hungarian Empire and Italy and had changed hands three times during the war.

Thousands died in the fierce fighting for possession of Gorizia. Only in Belgium had Hetty seen such terrible destruction. She described Gorizia's ancient fortress as looking as 'one would imagine Edinburgh Castle would do after a heavy bombardment from Arthur's Seat.'

There were horrific sights in Gorizia's historic cemetery, where barbed-wire, trenches and gun emplacements had been set up during the fighting. Shells fired into the cemetery by the Italians had disturbed graves and family vaults, exposing the coffins and their occupants in a hideous scene of resurrection. The cemetery had some new occupants, Austrian officers and men buried 'in painfully neat rows.'

Hetty was far-sighted as to what might happen to these Adriatic provinces now that the Austro-Hungarian Empire was passing into history and it had yet to be decided 'where Italian rule should end and that of the new Jugo-Slav [sic] state begin.'

> German-speaking masters were obviously out of place, but there is no question here but that the Slovene element is very strong and only those who know them best can really estimate the sources of trouble between the Jugo-Slavs [sic] themselves and their possible capacity for forming and ruling a large empire.

Talks on the proposed new Yugoslavian state had begun in October 1918 in what is now Ljubljana, capital of Slovenia. Back then it was mostly known by its German name of Laibach. Observing that in Ljubljana, less than 40 miles from Gorizia, the 'Serbs and Croats were already at each other's throats,' Hetty added:

> Even the youngest of us have known several Balkan wars, and it seems likely that some time will elapse before the Dalmatic and Albanian coast, with all its heterogeneous hinterland, settles into permanent peace.

She worked in one of the hospitals here for a few weeks, finding it odd to be using bed linen and temperature charts marked in German, from when it had been an Austrian military hospital. The workload was not nearly so heavy and she had time to visit 'the lovely city of Trieste.' She doesn't say how she got back to Britain but she might have been waiting for a berth on a troop or hospital ship leaving the Adriatic port.

Trieste had been a prize in the territorial dispute

between Italy and the Austro-Hungarian Empire. In 1915, the secret Treaty of London promised the Italian government most of those provinces it regarded as 'unredeemed Italy' in return for unconditional military support to the Allies of Britain, France and Russia.

As peace gradually took hold, Hetty wished she could forget she was a nurse and become a traveller again, but this how she ends her wartime memoir:

> And yet I do not think I could bear to be in any of these countries which have suffered so much in this long struggle without having some work to do in helping the people. There will probably be plenty of that for all of us for many a long day to come.

And then, at last, it was time for her to go home. She left Gorizia in February 1919.

PART III

The Writing

10

A Literary Partnership

Alistair My Brother

Henrietta Tayler's memoir of the First World War, *A Scottish Nurse at Work*, was published by the Bodley Head in London in their *On Active Service* series in 1920. By this time she'd settled back into post-war life. She enjoyed living in London, as she also enjoyed frequent visits out of the city, heading both north and south.

There was a cottage at each end of the country, one in Banff and one in West Sussex, in the village of Angmering-on-Sea. The Angmering house was called Duff Cottage. Given that the Taylers had strong connections with Sussex, this may have been a family property.

Hetty and Alistair did a lot of their writing at Duff Cottage in Angmering. Trips to Banff kept them in touch with life in Rothiemay, Glenbarry, Aberdeen and North East Scotland. Much of the research required for their books took them to those charter rooms in houses and castles still owned by their numerous relatives. There were meetings with publishers, field clubs and antiquarian societies.

Brother and sister had published their first joint, full-length work just before the war, in 1914. Building on the family and subsequent wider local success of *The Book of the Duffs*, in 1920 they published *Records of the County of Banff 1660–1760*. The publisher was the New Spalding Club of Aberdeen, one of several of those antiquarian societies and field clubs around the country dedicated to researching and preserving Scotland's history. The Taylers wrote articles and edited historical manuscripts for many of them, including The Roxburghe Club and The Scottish History Society.

Over the 1920s, Alistair and Henrietta jointly published five books. In the 1930s, they published thirteen, while Hetty published two on her own and one – *The Jacobite Court at Rome in 1719* – with the confusingly named Baron Alexander Forbes Forbes. Alistair and Henrietta's publishers included Milne & Hutchison of Aberdeen, Constable of Edinburgh, Thomas Nelson, John Murray and Oliver & Boyd of London. Their books were well publicised and garnered good reviews. One reviewer praised their book on the 1715 Rising for its 'searching realism.'

They may have had an advantage with Constable of Edinburgh. One of their Duff cousins ran it for many years up until his death in 1928. Walter Biggar Blaikie was also a highly-respected authority on the Jacobites and the 1745 Jacobite Rising.

It's hard to say how Alistair and Henrietta's literary partnership worked. Contemporary newspaper reports in those more sexist times often present Alistair, the

Laird of Glenbarry, as the great historian, with his devoted sister as his assistant and helpmeet. To be fair, she herself may have encouraged this. Always preferring to work away in the background, she was never a woman who sought the limelight.

Become familiar with the Taylers' work and you get the sense that Alistair helped a lot with the research but that Hetty did most, if not all, of the writing. If you look at the books she published on her own, the lively and immediate style is certainly very much that of the joint works. She also had a penchant for italics and exclamation marks when she wanted to hammer home a point. Alistair's solo efforts, while scholarly and meticulously researched, are rather more stolid and generally a lot less lively in style.

Hetty herself was always scrupulous about giving her brother his place. There's the occasional comment from a friend suggesting she may have given Alistair a little too much credit. It's clear however that she greatly valued his lively sense of humour — always useful when you're deep in a seemingly never-ending research and writing project — and his keen eye. Perhaps they shared the research, she wrote it up and he offered his critique.

It's obvious that they both loved the thrill of the chase of historical research. They delighted in turning up nuggets of information, especially those other researchers hadn't yet found, and presenting them in a coherent and readable narrative.

In 1928, they did exactly that in one of their most

HENRIETTA TAYLER

important and enduringly useful works, *Jacobites of Aberdeenshire and Banffshire in the Forty-Five.*

important and enduringly useful works, *Jacobites of Aberdeenshire and Banffshire in the Forty-Five.*

11

A Passion for Jacobites

*It takes a real Scot
to know that Aberdeen is Lowland!*

Hetty and Alistair dedicated *Jacobites of Aberdeenshire and Banffshire in the Forty-Five* to Walter Biggar Blaikie, their cousin and noted Jacobite scholar.

> By special permission, obtained during
> the last week of his life, this book is
> affectionately dedicated to the memory of
> WALTER BIGGAR BLAIKIE, LL.D., D.L.,
> The greatest authority on the Forty-Five,
> By his cousins, the authors,
> ALISTAIR TAYLER AND
> HENRIETTA TAYLER,
> at Duff Cottage,
> Angmering-on-Sea,
> in Sussex,
> July 11, 1928.

In 1897, Blaikie had published the *Itinerary of Prince Charles Edward Stuart*, detailing the Prince's movements around Scotland and into England in 1745–46. In 1916 he edited and presented several contemporary documents under the title of *Origins of the Forty-Five*. This remains one of the pillars of Jacobite scholarship. Throughout his life he collected pamphlets, prints, rare books and Jacobite memorabilia. The Blaikie Collection is now in the National Library of Scotland in Edinburgh, donated by his daughters.

Blaikie and his cousins were part of a group of historians writing from the middle of the 19th century onwards about the 1745 Jacobite Rebellion. In 1840 a boost had been given to Jacobite studies by the publication of *History of the Rebellion of 1745–46* by Robert Chambers. This was largely based on *The Lyon in Mourning* by Bishop Robert Forbes.

The Lyon in Mourning is the collective name given to the contents of ten small leather-bound notebooks crammed full of eye-witness and contemporary reports of the events of the '45. Copied from letters and recorded from interviews, this testimony was compiled by Bishop Forbes while it was still an act of treason to demonstrate support for the Jacobite Cause. They contain a scrap of material from the dress Bonnie Prince Charlie wore when he was disguised as Flora MacDonald's maidservant and a fragment of wood from an oar of the boat in which he travelled over the sea to Skye. The original handwritten notebooks are also now in the National Library of Scotland.

In 1895 the Scottish History Society published Bishop Forbes' *The Lyon in Mourning* in its entirety. This was another huge boost to Jacobite scholars. The Taylers described it as 'this valuable storehouse.' *The Lyon in Mourning* and the many other papers to which they had access through their family connections helped complete the jigsaw of information which allowed closer and more accurate analysis and sometimes re-interpretation of the '45. The Taylers seized every opportunity offered to do so. They had one very specific point to make in *Jacobites of Aberdeenshire and Banffshire in the Forty-Five*.

Histories of the '45 tended to imply the drama had played out only in the Highlands. By detailing hundreds of those who went out for Charles Edward Stuart in Aberdeenshire and Banffshire, Alistair and Henrietta's aim was to dispel that notion. Proud as they always were of their Scottish ancestry and credentials, they delighted in declaring that only a real Scot would know that Aberdeen was, culturally and historically, part of the Lowlands.

In many of their other books the Taylers were very much editors, albeit extremely well-informed ones, adding footnotes and comments to contemporary letters and documents. *Jacobites of Aberdeenshire and Banffshire in the Forty-Five* does contain lots of letters and extracts from letters but there's much more original writing in this book.

The first hundred pages is a round-up and analysis of the situation in North East Scotland in 1745 and after. This is followed by three hundred pages of an alphabetical list of those involved on the Jacobite side. Brother and sister pointed out that a great deal of support had come from the Episcopalian and Catholic families of the area and that:

> In common with the rest of Scotland, Aberdeen and Banff had not received the benefits which had been promised by the Act of Union, and the grievance of being largely governed from London was still great.

Alistair and Henrietta established by their researches that the Aberdeenshire and Banffshire Jacobites of 1745 had made up one-sixth of Bonnie Prince Charlie's fighting men. They were cock-a-hoop to have proved their point.

> Our "Nor-east" corner, cold and bleak though it may be in parts, was found capable of the warmest enthusiasm and the most enduring loyalty, not only to its Prince, but to its lairds, as is shown by the stories of Lord Pitsligo, Moir of Stoneywood, Gordon of Blelack and others.

As was often the case, many of those they wrote about in *Jacobites of Aberdeenshire and Banffshire in the Forty-Five* sat upon one of the abundant branches of their own family tree. Some of their Duff and other forbears went out for Bonnie Prince Charlie, others were strongly pro-Hanoverian. One was the boy whose own father hadn't recognized him as one of his 36 children. Captain Robert Duff commanded the aptly named *HMS Terror*, harrying the West Highlands and the Hebrides during the hunt for the fugitive Bonnie Prince Charlie and making vicious reprisal raids after Culloden and the failure of the rising.

Alistair and Henrietta noted in their introduction to *Jacobites of Aberdeenshire and Banffshire in the Forty-Five* the many sources from which they had drawn their information, such as the Public Record Office in London, the British Museum and Register House in Edinburgh. They had also relied 'very largely upon private correspondence and family records and traditions preserved in the district, which they have made it their business to collect during many years past.'

Their thanks for access to these private papers include a few fellow historians and scholars. Most of the 36 names on their list give us a roll call of the gentry of North East Scotland in the late 1920s. They include the wonderfully named Cavendish Abercromby, Alice Lady Forbes, Duffs, Gordon Duffs and the Countess of Seafield.

They – somehow it sounds like Hetty – always noticed the small domestic details, like how many of the cash-strapped Scottish Jacobite exiles in Rome got together to eat their midday meal so as to share the cost, 'having perhaps only a piece of bread and a glass of wine at night.'

The hardships she'd endured while nursing in war-torn Europe had made her aware of how food being in short supply could alter how you arranged your day. She drew a parallel with Jacobite times and her own, recording of some Jacobite exiles who fled to Europe in 1746:

> Others started small market gardens in various parts of France (quaintly reminiscent of ex-officers after the

Great War.) They do not seem to have been very successful, but at least the produce helped to feed their
numerous families, which continued to increase wherever
they went. Duncan Robertson of Struan is found saying
how gladly he would exchange the grapes he grows for
the blaeberrries of his native land.

Fascinated and moved though they were by the Jacobites,
particularly those of 1745, the Taylers were clear-eyed
about Jacobitism as a political movement and the sorry
end to the life of Prince Charles Edward Stuart, who
died an alcoholic in Rome in 1788. In her introduction
to *Jacobite Epilogue*, published in 1941, Hetty quoted
Robert Burns' description of those who were out in the
'45, the men who 'shook hands with ruin for what they
esteemed the cause of their King and Country.'

> In the following year also there came to the throne in
> England the first British-born prince of the new dynasty,
> George III; the *fait accompli* was gradually accepted
> and Jacobitism as a militant factor soon passed away,
> though sentimentally it persisted for nearly thirty years
> more until the death in Rome of the weary old man
> who had once been "Bonnie Prince Charlie."

Interestingly, one of their neighbours in Angmering-on-
Sea was a latter-day Jacobite. Francis Skeet was also a
devout Catholic and a descendant of several Northum-
brian families. The combination was a common one in
the 18th century. There were many in Northumberland
and elsewhere in the North of England who maintained
their loyalty to the Catholic Church and the Stuarts.

Many men of these families rallied to the Jacobite Cause in 1715, as some did also in 1745.

What was out of the ordinary was that in the 20th century Skeet seriously believed there should and could be a restoration to the British throne of the House of Stuart. The line had descended through to the Royal House of Bavaria and the Jacobite heir in the 1930s was Crown Prince Rupprecht. He was of the House of Wittelsbach, the family to which Elisabeth, Queen of the Belgians also belonged. Rupprecht himself discouraged supporters such as Skeet, as the current House of Wittelsbach lays no claim to the British throne.

Skeet also wrote about Jacobites and Jacobitism, mainly in books concentrating on his own forebears and associated English North Country families. However, one of his books was a biography of Bonnie Prince Charlie's only acknowledged child, Charlotte Stuart, Duchess of Albany. Charlotte was the daughter of the Prince's long-term mistress, Clementine Walkinshaw. As an illegitimate child, neither Charlotte nor her own three illegitimate children could be legitimate Stuart heirs.

Henrietta Tayler wrote about Charlotte Stuart too. *Prince Charlie's Daughter* was published twenty years after Skeet's book and is based on a resource he hadn't used, Charlotte's letters to her mother. These had been deposited in Oxford's Bodleian Library in the same year that Skeet published his biography of Charlotte.

Hetty was pretty scathing about Skeet and his book. She was critical of his 'reverence and almost adulation' of Charlotte, his treatment of her as a 'Catholic heroine' and according her the title of Her Royal Highness, 'which she actually was not.' Hetty also wrote that Skeet's translations from French of some of the papers he did consult, 'are sometimes so free as to be misleading.' The accomplished linguist was clearly appalled at this carelessness.

Skeet's espousal of the Jacobite Cause nearly two hundred years after Culloden puts him way out on the fringes of political thought in the early 20th century. Whether a Stuart or a Hanoverian sat on the British throne was a matter of supreme irrelevance to Socialists, Red Clydesiders and supporters of the Scottish Home Rule movement.

Many Scots maintained a sentimental attachment to the Stuarts expressed through song and story, but that was all it was. The growing support for Home Rule for Scotland had very little to do with Bonnie Prince Charlie and the Jacobites. Some of us might now beg to differ as to the relevance of the events of 1745-46 to modern politics but that's another story.

Hetty did encounter one other latter-day Jacobite. She gave him short shrift when he wrote to her seeking support for the repeal of the Act of Settlement. This is the legislation that prevents a Roman Catholic from succeeding to the British throne. Passed in 1701, it was specifically designed to bar the Catholic Stuarts. Hetty wrote a stiff letter in reply to the plea to join the campaign against this legislation, saying she could never be associated with 'any movement so subversive as to repeal the Act of Settlement.'

Hetty and Alistair were living through the high tide of Britishness, cemented as that was going to be by the gargantuan joint effort required to defeat Nazi Germany during the Second World War. They belonged to a family which had climbed high through seizing opportunities presented first by the political Union of Scotland and England and subsequently by those offered by the British Empire. Their grandmother Helen was born in Calcutta, the daughter of a Scottish surgeon to the East India Company. Their cousin Walter Biggar Blaikie spent three years as a civil engineer in India, also working for the East India Company.

Their cousin Alexander Duff, now 1st Duke of Fife, had married Louise, daughter of Edward VII. Louise was now the Princess Royal. Her two daughters by the Duke of Fife had been granted the title of Princess by their great-grandmother Queen Victoria. Henrietta and Alistair were closely related to British royalty, and not of the fugitive Jacobite variety.

As far as they were concerned, the Taylers were both Scottish and British: and attitudes were different back then. When Alistair matriculated at Oxford University, he gave his address as Rothiemay House, N.B. The initials stand for North Britain. Railway hotels in both Edinburgh and Glasgow were called *The North British* up until the 1960s. Today they have different names. No Scot nowadays would ever say that they come from North Britain.

Alistair and Henrietta's love for their native Banff-shire was deep and genuine, as was their admiration for their forebears and the Jacobites of the late 17th and first half of the 18th centuries. All the evidence suggests that their sympathies were not with Jacobitism as a political cause but with the loyalty and sacrifices of those who supported it.

12

Labours of Love

The amiable Lord Pitsligo.

On Halloween 1929, the Aberdeen Press and Journal informed its readers that 'Miss Henrietta Tayler, sister of the laird of Glenbarry' had just published a guidebook to Arles in France, illustrated by her sister Mrs Blenkinsopp Coulson. Miss Tayler had also 'just gone off for a short holiday in Avignon with her sister, who winters there.' The P & J further informed its readers that Hetty was 'hard at work on her next Jacobite book.'

An English Guide to Arles and Neighbourhood, price two shillings or ten francs, was short but comprehensive, with a colourful cover, 36 black and white illustrations and two maps sketched by Constance. Showing that the British fondness for Provence goes back a long way, Hetty recommended several other works in English on the charm of the area.

The Tayler sisters' guidebook was dedicated to Monsieur le Docteur Morizot, mayor of Arles, and his wife Madame Morizot, 'in grateful recognition of kindness received.'

Hetty's guide to Arles was not like a modern guidebook,

with recommendations on where to stay and where to eat. Instead, it offered information for the scholarly traveller, concentrating on the long history of Arles and the magnificence of its varied and historic architecture.

There is no mention of Van Gogh, who painted some of his most well-known works in Arles in the 1870s, or of his fellow artist and host there, Paul Gauguin. Constance was an artist. Hetty sketched and had waxed lyrical in her wartime memoir about how the light at De Panne playing on sand dunes, sky and sea attracted so many artists there. Leaving Van Gogh out of the guidebook to Arles seems a curious omission.

In 1931, she presented a copy of *Arles: The English Guidebook* to Aberdeen University. The University Library holds this copy and one other she gave to her friend and fellow historian Malcolm Bulloch. Among other works, Bulloch wrote *The House of Gordon*, the defining study of that clan and family.

In her covering letter to him, Hetty wrote that she didn't suppose such a short effort was worthy of a review. The tone's a wee bit wistful. Clearly, like all writers, she always wanted to know what readers thought of her books.

The productive Alistair and Hetty published two books in 1930, the year after Hetty went off to Avignon with their sister Constance. *Morayshire MPs Since the Act of Union* was published by Yeadon's, an old-established bookseller's in Elgin in Morayshire. The Jacobite book mentioned by the Press and Journal was *Jacobite Letters to Lord Pitsligo, 1745–46.* It shines a spotlight on one of the most attractive personalities of the 1745 Jacobite Rising.

Alexander Forbes, 4th Lord Pitsligo, was 67 years old when he left his home near Fraserburgh in North East Scotland to join Charles Edward Stuart's army at Edinburgh in September 1745. Pitsligo was a gentleman and a scholar, an author, an early advocate of education for girls and women and a convivial man, who had many friends. Pitsligo's Horse was a cavalry regiment, numbering between 100–200 gentlemen and their servants.

In their brief biography of him which prefaces his letters, the Taylers recount how Lord Pitsligo paused before setting off, took off his hat and said, 'Lord, thou knowest our Cause is just. Gentlemen, march.' When he rode into the Jacobite camp at Duddingston on the outskirts of Edinburgh, a contemporary observer said it was as though religion, virtue and justice came in with 'this venerable old man.'

Lord Pitsligo survived Culloden. Although he remained a fugitive for the rest of his life, he was hidden and protected by his friends and tenants and died in bed at his son's house at the age of 84.

In their preface to the book, Alistair and Henrietta wrote that other historians had been ignorant of this packet of letters they were printing for the first time. They always loved to steal a march on their research rivals. They did have an unfair advantage here. Probably only historians as well-connected as they were would have found the letters. They had fetched up at Fettercairn House in Kincardineshire, passed down to Lord Clinton, a several times great-nephew of Lord Pitsligo.

As usual, brother and sister put the letters into context, adding footnotes and brief biographies of the main correspondents. Editing these letters to the 'amiable Lord Pitsligo' had been, so they wrote, a labour of love.

Their enthusiasm for raking through the document boxes of their relatives continued unabated. *Jacobites of Aberdeenshire and Banffshire in the Rising of 1715* was published by Oliver and Boyd in 1934. It was dedicated to Malcolm Bulloch, to whom Hetty had given a copy of her guidebook to Arles.

The '15 was a much shorter affair than the '45 and fizzled out at the indecisive Battle of Sheriffmuir. The research for it was harder, as the information was more difficult to find. Much incriminating material had been 'prudently destroyed' not long after the conflict. Nevertheless, Hetty and Alistair managed to present information on hundreds of those who came out for the Stuarts in 1715.

As ever, they brought these people leaping off the page. One example is the black humour a young Jacobite soldier deployed against himself. Nineteen years old in 1715, John Urquhart of Knockleith, later of Craigston, left a list of the dangers he had escaped and the blessings he had received. The former, all happening during the '15, included being bitten by an otter, falling from a high rock and being thrown from and crushed under his horse in the middle of a blizzard. Despite suffering more calamities during his life, including nearly drowning off Shetland, John Urquhart died in his bed in Banff in 1756 at the age of 60.

Once again, Alistair and Henrietta took the opportunity to emphasize the hugely significant role North East Scotland had played in the Jacobite rebellions, especially the '45. They mentioned this again in the preface to *Jacobites of Aberdeenshire and Banffshire in the Rising of 1715*. Long after publication of the companion volume on the '45 they had found a letter written a month after Culloden from one opponent of the Jacobites to another.

"In our parts, Lord Pitsligo with the other Aberdeenshire and Banffshire Lairds *and their people*, a very few excepted, did more harm since this Rebellion began than all the Highlanders put together." This adds contemporary support to the now proved fact of the prominent part taken by this district in the Rising of 1745.

It was a point Alistair and Henrietta Tayler never tired of making.

13

Making the Most Thrilling Discoveries

The uncharted seas of the Stuart Papers.

In 1934 Hetty and Alistair turned their attention to the Stuart Papers at Windsor. These had been bought by the British royal family even before the death of Bonnie Prince Charlie's younger brother Henry. He was a cardinal of the Roman Catholic Church and the last legitimate heir of the Royal Stuarts. It was the British Prince Regent, later George IV, who took an interest in the papers of the branch of his family that had tried to unseat his grandfather. He also arranged for an annual British pension to be paid to the Cardinal, which Henry benefited from during his final years.

One of those who had previously drawn attention to the existence of the Stuart Papers was the British Ambassador to Italy in the 1780s, Sir William Hamilton, husband of the infamous Emma, mistress of Admiral Lord Nelson. Nelson was to personally carry the papers back to England on the Victory but his death at Trafalgar prevented that. The archive arrived in Windsor two years' later, in 1807, and became the property of the British crown.

Bound into over 500 volumes, the letters and papers had remained unindexed for over a century. Nothing daunted, Alistair and Henrietta plunged in. The introduction to their resulting book, *The Stuart Papers at Windsor*, is robustly scathing about how many historians had declined to tackle the papers.

> But among the hundreds of historians, of memoir writers and of novelists who have dealt with the eighteenth century and particularly with the Jacobite Risings and the protagonists in them, those who have made really practical use of this collection could be counted on the fingers of both hands. A list of those who seem, as far as the present writers can ascertain, to have drawn *any* real material, however small, directly from them, will be found on page 37. The number who have not done so, and would thereby have avoided many of the errors into which they have fallen, is *legion*.

Even their esteemed cousin Walter Biggar Blaikie, described in the preface as 'the eminent Jacobite historian,' comes in for criticism. He took some of the letters second-hand from another historian *'and quoted Browne's errors.'* Dr Blaikie never even went in person to consult the Stuart Papers in the Windsor archives. You can feel Hetty's shock at any scholar not making the effort to see the original letters and documents.

The Taylers did not think the indexing was necessarily to be welcomed. They were proud to have been the last historians 'to sail the uncharted seas of the Stuart Papers, making on the way the most thrilling discoveries.'

Foremost among these thrilling discoveries was a slim volume which has been of enormous value and interest to students of the '45.

In *1745 And After*, Alistair and Henrietta presented the journal of John William O'Sullivan while he was in Scotland with Prince Charles Edward Stuart in 1745–46. Hetty was over the moon when she and Alistair discovered O'Sullivan's diary and realized how many other researchers had missed it. She loved the detective work involved in researching and was always interested in how papers got to the libraries and archives in which they eventually rested.

O'Sullivan was one of the Seven Men of Moidart, those who were with Bonnie Prince Charlie when he made landfall in Scotland in the summer of 1745. An Irish Catholic from County Kerry, he spent much of his childhood in France. Destined for the priesthood, he chose to become a soldier instead, fighting with the French army in Corsica, Italy and on the Rhine. In Corsica, O'Sullivan learned how a guerrilla army fought. In Italy he learned how to deploy guerrilla tactics.

This experience recommended O'Sullivan to Charles Edward Stuart. Meeting the Irishman in Europe a year or so before the '45, Charles found him to also be a congenial companion. Others around the Prince detested O'Sullivan. To this day, he remains a controversial figure.

His journal is a fascinating document. While his handwriting was legible, his spelling was diabolically bad, even by 18th century standards. As I have written elsewhere, this can afford the modern researcher much innocent amusement in what can often be a poignant subject. Reading about not the *Duke* but the *Duck* of Cumberland can raise the mood.

Hetty described O'Sullivan's spelling as 'original' — you can hear her saying that, amused eyebrows raised — but observed that did not stop the reader from knowing to which places in Scotland he was referring. Nor does it stop us from knowing what the Prince and his men ate for their dinner. On 14th September 1745, for example, Charles:

> …halted at Banacburn, dined at Sr Hugh Paterson's, & sent to the Town of Sterling ordering them, to send so many barrels of Bear, bread, Chees, &ca, to refraish his men, wch they did.

O'Sullivan's diary also gives us the corroboration of someone who was there of the ball held at Holyroodhouse in Edinburgh in the autumn of 1745. This was after the Jacobite victory in September of that year at the Battle of Prestonpans. For six heady weeks, Bonnie Prince Charlie and his army occupied Edinburgh, Charles holding court in the palace of his ancestors at the foot of the Royal Mile.

Female support for the Jacobite Cause being significant in terms of influence, moral, financial and practical support, it was decided to throw a 'ball for the Ladys.' Although Charles went along with the idea, attended and was polite, he would not dance and withdrew early.

Dismayed, some of his officers followed him and asked why he would not dance when they knew he loved to do so. They had organized the ball as much for him as for the ladies. This is how O'Sullivan described Charles' response.

> "Its very true, says the Prince, & am very glad to see the Lady's and yu divert yr selfs, but I have now another Air to dance, until that be finished I'll dance no other." It was very strange yt a Prince of that age who really liked dancing, & fowling, never thought of any pleasures, and was as retired as a man of sixty.

As ever, the editors of *1745 and After* presented O'Sullivan's Journal with illuminating footnotes and context. The Taylers' years of research and knowledge of their subject shines through. In their own day, they were well known and acknowledged experts on those *The Times* later called 'the Jacobite partisans' of the 18th century.

1745 And After was published as a joint work by Thomas Nelson & Sons in June 1938. The publisher's London offices were in Paternoster Row near St Paul's Cathedral. This gives us a nice connection to the anti-Jacobite propaganda pamphlets of 1745–46, churned out in panicked response to the threat posed by Bonnie Prince Charlie and his advancing army, the terrifying hordes of 'bare-arsed banditti' who were heading for London.

One of the busiest of those deploying the black arts of propaganda was novelist Henry Fielding, author of

Tom Jones. Many of his pamphlets were published by Mary Cooper of Paternoster Row, then at the heart of bookselling and publishing. In the lee of St Paul's Cathedral, the old street was obliterated in the Blitz of the Second World War, although its line and name survives in the modern buildings which stand there now.

Alistair and Henrietta' researches through the Stuart Papers at Windsor produced three books in total: *1745 and After, The Stuart Papers at Windsor* and *Jacobite Epilogue: a Further Selection from the Stuart Papers at Windsor.*

14

Man and Woman about Town

*The honorary aunt of innumerable families
in Scotland and England.*

Alistair and Henrietta led an active social life. They
crop up in the Society columns of newspapers as guests
at the parties and weddings of friends and family. The
newspapers of the time listed the wedding presents
Society couples received. Hetty sometimes gave them a
cheque. More frequently she gave the bride a nice piece
of jewellery, a 'diamond arrow brooch', a 'Cairngorm
heart with gold chain', a 'diamond and emerald ring'.

Both brother and sister were comfortably off, from
inherited family money and investments rather than
their books. Hetty liked to have nice things around her,
paintings, jewellery and antiques.

In London Alistair was most definitely a man about
town, with a high-powered circle of friends. In 1934 Sir
Compton Mackenzie was unable to check the proofs of
his *Prince Charlie and His Ladies* 'owing to an unexpected
journey to South America.' Sounds like he led an
interesting life. Sir Compton was grateful to Alistair for

taking on the job for him, despite having to wrestle with what Mackenzie himself described as his 'pestilential handwriting.'

Alistair was a member of the prestigious Garrick Club, named in honour of 18th century actor David Garrick. This social and dining club in London's West End was set up as a meeting place where gentlemen interested in the theatre and literature could meet actors and writers.

One of Alistair's closest friends and fellow Garrick Club member was novelist and playwright Arnold Bennett. Famous for his novels set in the Potteries, the six towns which together make up Stoke-on-Trent, Bennett was a hugely successful author, a celebrity of the 1920s. He even has a supper dish named after him: *Omelette Arnold Bennett*. It was created for him by the Savoy Hotel Grill and is still served there today: eggs, smoked haddock, Parmesan cheese and cream.

Bennett died in 1931, leaving the then huge sum of £100,000. As the sole executor, Alistair was involved in a three-year-long legal tussle between Arnold Bennett's widow and his long-term partner.

More happily, Alistair had a passion for the theatre. With Arnold Bennett and old Oxford chum Nigel Playfair, he was a director of the Lyric Theatre in Hammersmith. Playfair was a famous actor-manager. When he took over the Lyric in 1918, everyone thought he was mad.

Hammersmith was the 'Far West', miles away from Shaftesbury Avenue and the West End where all the other theatres were. That wasn't the only problem. The Lyric was in a sorry state. The locals called it 'The Blood-and-Flea-Pit.' In an engaging history he wrote of his theatre, Playfair pointed out that this also made it cheap.

Operating on a shoestring budget, the Lyric was reborn, with Arnold Bennett as chairman and Playfair as director and producer. As co-director, they elected 'Mr Alistair Tayler, whose combination of enthusiasm with a talent for figures is hardly excelled even by that of Bennett.' Playfair also praised Alistair's shrewdness and pointed out that neither he nor Arnold Bennett made much material profit as a result of their input.

The Lyric confounded the nay-sayers. Throughout the 1920s and early 1930s the theatre staged highly success-ful plays, pantomimes and operettas. On New Year's Eve 1922, *Polly* went down a storm at London's Kingsway theatre, having already played for well over a year at the Lyric.

This sequel to John Gay's *The Beggar's Opera* had been jazzed-up with a new libretto and modern music. One critic compared it favourably to Gilbert & Sullivan and commented on the delight of Mr Alistair Tayler, 'the Laird of Glenbarry,' as he watched the performance sitting in a box next to Arnold Bennett. Hetty loved the theatre and always supported her brother in his endeavours, so there can be little doubt that she too enjoyed the productions at the Lyric.

Alistair and Henrietta continued to visit Banffshire, staying at their cottage in Banff and keeping in touch with relatives and friends who shared their antiquarian interests. For almost two decades, Alistair made a point of delivering a paper every year on some aspect of local history or genealogy to the Banffshire Field Club. In March 1937, Hetty gave the paper, Alistair unable to attend due to an attack of lumbago.

In the summer of 1939, Henrietta gave a special prize at the Glenbarry Picnic and Games to the best Highland dancer under twelve. Sadly, by this time she was there on her own.

Alastair Tayler died in November 1937. His death was sudden and unexpected, coming only a day after he'd returned to London from a visit north. His friends were shocked. His sister was devastated. She was there when he died of a heart attack at their flat in Kensington's Queen's Gate.

She had always given her beloved brother his due and continued to do so. She made a point of acknowledging how much he had contributed to the research and compiling of those joint works which appeared after he died.

The Stuart Papers at Windsor was published in 1939 as a second posthumous work for Alistair. Again, Hetty wrote warmly of him in the preface to the book.

The task of selecting, transcribing and annotating these was necessarily a very long and absorbing one and has taken over three years. Owing to the sudden death of my brother in November 1937, I am left to complete it alone, without the benefit of his very careful eye and acute sense of humour and fitness. It is, however, still a joint work.

She kept going, as she always did, and paid a simple but heartfelt tribute to her beloved brother and literary partner in *Jacobite Epilogue*, published in 1941:

DEDICATED
TO THE MEMORY OF
ALISTAIR
MY BROTHER

15

In a Happy Hour

We had many eighteenth century
acquaintances in common.

Henrietta Tayler was 70 at the start of the Second
World War. She helped out where she could, sometimes
in a very personal way. Two days before Christmas
1939, in the first winter of the war, she came to the
rescue of a young couple having a small wartime
wedding before the groom joined his regiment. Hetty
threw them a reception at her home in Kensington. The
bride wore red and carried a posy of Christmas roses.

In July 1943 Hetty was in Aberdeen, helping man
the white elephant stall at a War Comforts Fair, where
advice was being given on how best to stretch wartime
rations to provide meals for the family. One of the
'ingenious tips' was how to make 'a mildly alcoholic
drink from water, a yeast tablet and some sugar.' Just
the ticket to steady your nerves while the bombs were
dropping.

After the war she continued to travel between
London, Scotland and Sussex. She attended weddings,
christenings and birthday parties, kept up with old

friends and made new ones. She loved good conversation and was a fast and entertaining talker, always with lots of stories to tell.

She continued researching and writing until the end of her long life. Her final full-length book, the one based on the letters of Bonnie Prince Charlie's daughter Charlotte, was published in 1950, when she was 81. *Prince Charlie's Daughter* is as meticulously researched and tightly argued as ever, with lots of informed comment on the letters and the personalities involved.

Hetty died the following year, on 10th April 1951. *The Times* printed a handsome obituary two days later, (with a mistake in the year of Alistair's death).

Miss Henrietta Tayler, who died on Tuesday at her home in London at the age of 82, devoted much of her long life to research into the Jacobite partisans of the seventeenth and eighteenth centuries.

She approached her subject in a thoroughly scholarly manner and had the help of her brother, the late Alistair Tayler, until his death in 1939, in examining the great mass of original documents.

The obituary singles out a few titles for praise, including *1745 and After*, and also gives an admiring mention to *Prince Charlie's Daughter*.

...in her biography of Prince Charlie's daughter, Charlotte, published little more than 12 months ago, she discloses the fact that one of Charlotte's illegitimate children survived until 1854, and so "the end of an old song" had a more lingering cadence than had hitherto been supposed.

Sir James Fergusson of Kilkerran was a friend of Hetty's during her later years. He paid tribute to her in his foreword to her posthumously published *Two Accounts of the Escape of Prince Charles Edward*. Sir James was Keeper of the Records in Scotland and a researcher and writer on the Jacobites of 1745, most notably in *Argyle in the Forty-Five*. He wrote this of his friend and fellow Jacobite scholar.

> ...one of the charms of knowing her was that she made you free of a life and experience which ranged extra-ordinarily wide in people, places and epochs. We had many eighteenth-century acquaintances in common and in her conversation they were just as alive as contemporaries we both knew...

Sir James said that Hetty had more friends than anyone else he had ever met, young and old and stretching across the generations. He quoted her as saying, 'I always know people's grandfathers.' He ended his tribute by summing up Hetty and Alistair's contribution to Jacobite scholarship and with a touching portrait of Hetty at the end of her life. The Latin is a quote from Horace and can be rendered into English as: *He fell lamented by many good men.*

Their definitive history of the 'Fifteen, their editing of O'Sullivan's personal narrative of the 'Forty-Five, and Hetty's own editing of the anonymous History of the Rebellion for the Roxburghe Club would alone keep their names alive. But many, for years to come, who never read a history book, will remember Hetty as the tiny, shabby, smiling old lady who was the honorary aunt of innumerable families in Scotland and England. *Multis illa bonis flebibis occidit*; but she hardly knew a day's illness, and died, on 10 April, 1951, suddenly, without pain, and in a happy hour.

In her will she left jewellery, paintings and numerous generous financial bequests to relatives, god-children, friends, fellow scholars and charities. Further evidence that she worked right up till the end comes from *The Scottish Historical Review* of October 1951. It published the transcript of a letter she had sent them written by Angus MacDonell of Glengarry in November 1745.

Her commentary on this letter in the last article she ever wrote is classic Henrietta Tayler. Titled *Jacobite Rumours*, she's sure readers will remember it was MacDonell who commanded the Macdonalds of Glengarry in the 1745, despite being the second son and only 19 years old. He already had a son of his own and his wife was to bear him a posthumous daughter. He was accidentally shot dead by his own side in the streets of Falkirk after the Jacobites won that battle in January 1746. His daughter was named Angusia, in her dead father's honour. The letter was being published with the permission of the descendant who owned it.

Detailing as it does huge support for the Jacobite army which never materialized, including five thousand Spanish troops plus '...three hundred thousand Spanish pistols and arms for four thousand men more at White-haven,' Hetty's rebuke was as authoritative and acerbic as ever.

> It is pathetic to see the false reports and fairy stories with which the Prince's faithful Highlanders were misled; and one wonders how much young Angus had been dis-illusioned, as to the prospects of the cause, before his death two and a half months later.

The editor of the *Scottish Historical Review* added his tribute to Hetty at the bottom of her article and MacDonell's letter.

> Our readers will have learned with deep regret of the death of Miss Henrietta Tayler on 10 April 1951 at the age of 82. Miss Tayler's work is too well known to require recapitulation in the pages of this Review. Her death is a severe loss to Scottish historical study. But her many friends will take comfort in the knowledge that she was working and enjoying her work to the very last. This 'Document' was sent to the Editor on the day preceding her death with a short covering note expressing her intention to be in Edinburgh in May 'as usual.'

Helen Agnes Henrietta Tayler was buried in the Brompton Cemetery in Kensington in London in the same plot as her brother Alistair and their mother, Georgina, their father having been buried in Edinburgh. Sister Constance had died in 1948. The inscriptions for Hetty, Alistair and their mother are all simple, only their names and dates: modest to the last.

Enthusiasts for Jacobite history know and appreciate Henrietta and Alistair Tayler. Their work underpins so much of what we know about the people and events of 1715 and 1745. The Taylers' books continue to be cited in modern works by academic historians. Their meticulous rendering of original letters and documents and their years of knowledge of the subject have proved to be of enduring value. Unlike too many academic historians, their work is also highly readable.

Alistair and Henrietta Tayler themselves have stepped back and disappeared into the shadows. The old house at Rothiemay was demolished in the 1960s after a fire. A new Rothiemay House stands there now. Two original lodge houses and two stone gate-posts remain. The railway line still operates, transporting the travelling public between Aberdeen and Inverness, although the trains no longer stop at Rothiemay. The station building is long gone and nature has made a good job of reclaiming the platforms. In Spring, blazing yellow whin and broom bushes cover the old stones.

Crops still grow and sheep still graze in the surrounding fields. There are horses too, ridden now for leisure, not as a means of transport. The nearby antiquities endure: standing stones, carved Pictish stones, castles, ruined churches, chapels and lairds' houses, the stone circle at Rothiemay.

In a review in 1920 of her wartime memoir, *A Scottish Nurse at Work*, the reviewer praised Henrietta Tayler's vivid writing and ability to see the funny side in dark and difficult times, writing that her memoir demonstrated '...an unusual amount of pluck, grit, endurance and good temper in one woman.'

That sums her up beautifully. There is so much to admire in her life and personality. She was brave, intelligent, talented, witty and wise. She was always ready to help anyone who needed help. Working with her beloved brother Alistair, she contributed so much to our knowledge of Scottish history, particularly of the Jacobites of 1715 and 1745. She was a proud daughter of Banffshire and of Scotland.

This remarkable woman deserves to be remembered.

oOo

Select Bibliography

Banffshire Field Club, *The Papers of Alistair Tayler, 1924–37*, Banff, 1937

Duffy, Christopher, *The '45*, London, 2003

Gosling, Lucinda, *Knitting for Tommy: Keeping the Great War Soldier Warm*

Tayler, Henrietta, *A Scottish Nurse at Work* (On Active Service Series) Bodley Head, London, 1920

Thompson, Mark, *The White War: Life and Death on the Italian Front 1915–1919*, faber and faber, London, 2008

Books by Alistair & Henrietta Tayler, in chronological order of publication:

The Book of the Duffs W Brown, Edinburgh, 1914

Records of the County of Banff 1660–1760 New Spalding Club, Aberdeen, 1922

Lord Fife and his Factor (William Rose) Heinemann, London, 1925

The Domestic Papers of the Rose Family Milne & Hutchison, Aberdeen, 1926

Letters of John Orrok Milne & Hutchison, Aberdeen 1927

Jacobites of Aberdeenshire & Banffshire in the Forty-Five Milne & Hutchison, Aberdeen, 1928

Morayshire MPs Since the Act of Union JD Yeadon, Elgin, 1930

Jacobite Letters to Lord Pitsligo, 1745–46 Milne & Hutchinson, Aberdeen, 1930

The Jacobite Cess Roll for the County of Aberdeen in 1715 Aberdeen, 1932

The Valuation for the County of Aberdeen for the Year 1667 Third Spalding Club, Aberdeen, 1933

The Ogilvies of Boyne Aberdeen University Press, 1933

The Old Chevalier: James Francis Stuart Cassell, London, 1934

Jacobites of Aberdeenshire & Banffshire in the Rising of 1715 Oliver and Boyd, London, 1934

1715: The Story of the Rising Thomas Nelson, London, 1936

The House of Forbes Third Spalding Club, Aberdeen, 1937

A Jacobite Exile Alexander Maclehose & Co, London, 1937

1745 and After Thomas Nelson, London, 1938

John Graham of Claverhouse Duckworth, London, 1939

The Stuart Papers at Windsor John Murray, London, 1939

Jacobite Epilogue: a Further Selection from the Stuart Papers at Windsor Thomas Nelson, London, 1941

Books by Henrietta Tayler in collaboration with others:

The English Guidebook to Arles (with C Coulson)
The Garden City Press, Letchworth, 1929

The Jacobite Court at Rome in 1719 (with Baron Alexander Forbes Forbes) For the Scottish History Society, Edinburgh, 1938

Books and Some Papers by Henrietta Tayler alone:

A Scottish Nurse at Work (On Active Service series) Bodley Head, London, 1920

The House of Forbes Third Spalding Club, Aberdeen, 1937

Scotland's Child Sovereigns Constable, Edinburgh, 1937

History of the Family of Urquhart Aberdeen University Press, 1946

The Seven Sons of the Provost Thomas Nelson, London 1949

Lady Nithsdale and her Family L Drummond, London, 1949

Scotland's Child Sovereigns Constable, Edinburgh, 1937

Bonnie Prince Charlie (for younger readers) Thomas Nelson, London, 1945

A Jacobite Miscellany: Eight Original Papers on the Jacobite Rising of 1745–1746 Roxburghe Club, 1948

Prince Charlie's Daughter, being the Life and Letters of Charlotte of Albany Batchworth Press, London, 1950

Two Accounts of the Escape of Bonnie Prince Charlie, Oxford, Blackwell's for the Luttrell Society, 1951

Index

www.maggiecraig.co.uk

@CraigMaggie